On
Humour

'... steps with admirable adroitness from Tommy Cooper to Kant...
broaches a momentous subject with style and insight; there is no great
writer who is not humorous for some of the time.'

Terry Eagleton, *Radical Philosophy*

Praise for the series

"... allows a space for distinguished thinkers to write about their passions."
The Philosophers' Magazine

"... deserves high praise."
Boyd Tonkin, *The Independent* (UK)

"This is clearly an important series. I look forward to reading future volumes."
Frank Kermode, author of *Shakespeare's Language*

"... both rigorous and accessible."
Humanist News

"... the series looks superb."
Quentin Skinner

"... an excellent and beautiful series."
Ben Rogers, author of *A.J. Ayer: A Life*

"Routledge's *Thinking in Action* series is the throy junkie's answer to the eminently pocketable Penguin 60s series."
Mute Magazine (UK)

"Routledge's new series, *Thinking in Action*, brings philosophers to our aid ..."
Evening Standard (UK)

"... a welcome new series by Routledge."
Bulletin of Science, Technology and Society

SIMON CRITCHLEY

On
Humour

Routledge
Taylor & Francis Group

LONDON AND NEW YORK

First published 2002
by Routledge
2 Park Square, Milton Park, Abingdon, Oxon, OX14 4RN

Simultaneously published in the USA and Canada
by Routledge
270 Madison Ave, New York, NY 10016

Reprinted 2004, 2006 (three times), 2007, 2008 (twice), 2009, 2010

Routledge is an imprint of the Taylor & Francis Group, an informa business

© 2002 Simon Critchley

Typeset in Joanna and DIN by Keystroke, Jacaranda Lodge, Wolverhampton
Printed and bound in Great Britain by TJ International Ltd, Padstow, Cornwall

British Library Cataloguing in Publication Data
A catalogue record for this book is available from the British Library

Library of Congress Cataloging in Publication Data
A catalog record for this book has been requested

ISBN10 0–415–25120–6 (hbk)
ISBN10 0–415–25121–4 (pbk)

ISBN13 978–0–415–25120–4 (hbk)
ISBN13 978–0–415–25121–1 (pbk)

The bitter, the hollow and – haw! haw! – the mirthless. The bitter laugh laughs at that which is not good, it is the ethical laugh. The hollow laugh laughs at that which is not true, it is the intellectual laugh. Not good! Not true! Well, well. But the mirthless laugh is the dianoetic laugh, down the snout – haw! – so. It is the laugh of laughs, the *risus purus*, the laugh laughing at the laugh, the beholding, the saluting of the highest joke, in a word the laugh that laughs – silence please – at that which is unhappy.

Samuel Beckett, **Watt**

Introduction **One**   1

Three Theories of Humour   2
The Phenomenology of a Joke   3
Comic Timing   6
Laughter as an Explosion Expressed With the Body   7
Changing the Situation   9
Reactionary Humour   11
Structured Fun   12
Jokes: Good, Bad and Gulliver   14
Laughter's Messianic Power   16
Sensus and *Dissensus Communis*   18
Tristram Shandy, or Back to the Things Themselves   20

Is Humour Human? **Two**   25

Eccentric Humans   27
A Small Bestiary   29
Horace and Juvenal, Urbanity and Disgust   31
Outlandish Animals   34
Kant's Parrot   36

Laughing at Your Body – Post-Colonal Theory
Three   41

Being and Having   42
Physics and Metaphysics   43
Our Souls, Arseholes   45
Peditology   47
The Black Sun at the Centre of the Comic Universe   50

**The Laughing Machine – a Note on Bergson
and Wyndham Lewis Four 55**

A Cabbage Reading Flaubert – Now That's Funny 58
How Humour Begins in Philosophy 59

**Foreigners are Funny – the Ethicity and
Ethnicity of Humour Five 65**

The Universal and the Particular 66
Ethos and Ethnos 68
There was a Frenchman, an Englishman and
an Irishman . . . 71
Having the Courage of our Parochialism 73
Comic Repression 75

**The Joke's on All of Us – Humour as
Sensus Communis Six 79**

Shaftesbury's Reasonable Raillery 80
Disenchantment of Folly or Democratization of Wit? 83
Intersubjective Assent 85
Jokes as Everyday Anamnesis 86
Anaesthesia of the Heart 87
The Phenomenology of Phenomenology 88

**Why the Super-Ego is Your Amigo – My Sense of
Humour and Freud's Seven 93**

Finding Oneself Ridiculous 94
Subject as Abject Object 96
Melancholy Philosophers 98

Manic Intoxication 99

Humour as Anti-Depressant 101

Super-Ego I and II 102

Ideal Sickness 104

Laughter I and II 105

Smiling – the Mind's Mime 107

The *Risus Purus* 109

Notes 113

Bibliography 121

Thanks 125

Index 127

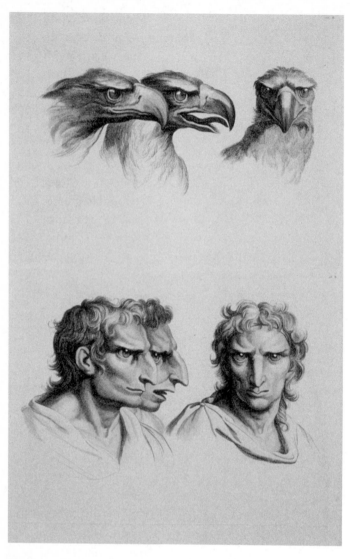

Three heads of an eagle and three heads of men in relation to the eagle
Source: Cnac-Mnam/Dist RMN. Charles Le Brun

Introduction

One

Human beings are troubled with the opinions (*dogmata*) they have of things, and not by the things themselves (*pragmata*).

Epictetus, as cited by Laurence Sterne

Jokes tear holes in our usual predictions about the empirical world. We might say that humour is produced by a disjunction between the way things are and the way they are represented in the joke, between expectation and actuality. Humour defeats our expectations by producing a novel actuality, by changing the situation in which we find ourselves. Examples are legion, from boy bishops reciting learned sermons, to talking dogs, hamsters and bears, to farting professors and incontinent ballerinas, to straight linguistic inversion: 'I could wait for you until the cows come home. On second thoughts, I'd rather wait for the cows until you come home'. Of course, this is hardly news. One already finds Cicero writing in *De Oratore*, 'The most common kind of joke is that in which we expect one thing and another is said; here our own disappointed expectation makes us laugh'. The comic world is not simply 'die verkehrte Welt', the inverted or upside-down world of philosophy, but rather the world with its causal chains broken, its social practices turned inside out, and common sense rationality left in tatters.

Of course, a similar tension between expectation and actuality might itself be claimed in the relation between the various objects of humour and any theoretical explanation thereof, the difference being that a theory of humour is not humorous. A joke explained is a joke misunderstood. In this case, what might make one laugh – albeit as dramatic irony – is the audacity or arrogance of the attempt to write a philosophy of humour. For example, persons who might not otherwise feel themselves to be experts in metapsychology or French spiritualism somehow feel confident in dismissing Freud's theory of jokes or Bergson's account of laughter because they are either not funny or simply miss the point. When it comes to what amuses us, we are all authorities, experts in the field. We know what we find funny. Such a claim to implicit or tacit knowledge is interesting in itself, for reasons that I will endeavour to spell out in a later chapter. However, the fact remains that humour is a nicely impossible object for a philosopher. But herein lies its irresistible attraction.

THREE THEORIES OF HUMOUR

In an effort to approach this nicely impossible object, I have been filling much of my time lately reading books on humour and laughter. As a glance at my bibliography will reveal, it is a surprisingly vast field, and much of the empirical research is extremely pleasurable. The further one looks, the more there is to see, not so much in philosophy, but more in the areas of history, literary history, theology and history of religion, sociology and anthropology.

There are many explanations of laughter and humour, that John Morreall does well to distill into three theories: the superiority theory, the relief theory and the incongruity theory.[1]

1 In the first theory, represented by Plato, Aristotle, Quintillian and, at the dawn of the modern era, Hobbes, we laugh from feelings of superiority over other people, from 'suddaine Glory arising from suddaine Conception of some Eminency

in our selves, by Comparison with the Infirmityes of others, or with our owne formerly'. Laughter is that 'passion, which hath no name', which would be forbidden to the virtuous guardians of Plato's imagined philosophical city. It is the superiority theory that dominates the philosophical tradition until the eighteenth century, and we shall have recourse to it in the discussion of ethnic humour.

2 The relief theory emerges in the nineteenth century in the work of Herbert Spencer, where laughter is explained as a release of pent-up nervous energy, but the theory is best known in the version given in Freud's 1905 book *Jokes and Their Relation to the Unconscious*, where the energy that is relieved and discharged in laughter provides pleasure because it allegedly economizes upon energy that would ordinarily be used to contain or repress psychic activity.

3 The incongruity theory can be traced to Francis Hutcheson's *Reflections Upon Laughter* from 1750, but is elaborated in related, but distinct, ways in Kant, as we shall see presently, Schopenhauer and Kierkegaard. As James Russell Lowell writes in 1870, 'Humour in its first analysis is a perception of the incongruous'. Humour is produced by the experience of a felt incongruity between what we know or expect to be the case, and what actually takes place in the joke, gag, jest or blague: 'Did you see me at Princess Diana's funeral? I was the one who started the Mexican wave'. Although I will discuss the other theories below, I would like to begin by exploring this idea of humour as incongruity.

THE PHENOMENOLOGY OF A JOKE

Can we describe what takes place in a joke? How might we give what philosophers call the 'phenomenology' of a joke? First, joking is a specific and meaningful practice that the audience and the joke-teller recognize as such. There is a tacit social contract at work here, namely some agreement about the social world in which we find ourselves as the implicit background to the joke. There has to be a sort of tacit consensus or implicit shared understanding as to what constitutes joking 'for us', as to which linguistic or visual routines are recognized as joking. That is, in order for the incongruity of the joke to be seen as such, there has to be a congruence between joke structure and social structure – no social congruity, no comic incongruity. When this implicit congruence or tacit contract is missing, then laughter will probably not result, which can be the experience of trying – and failing – to tell a joke in a foreign language. Bergson explains what he calls 'the leading idea in all our investigations' in *Le rire*:

> To understand laughter, we must put it back into its natural environment, which is society, and above all we must determine the utility of its function, which is a social one. [. . .] Laughter must answer to certain requirements of life in common. It must have a *social* signification.[2]

So, in listening to a joke, I am presupposing a social world that is shared, the forms of which the practice of joke-telling is going to play with. Joking is a game that players only play successfully when they both understand and follow the rules. Wittgenstein puts the point perspicuously,

> What is it like for people not to have the same sense of humour? They do not react properly to each other. It's as though there were a custom amongst certain people for one person to throw another a ball which he is supposed to catch and throw back; but some people, instead of throwing it back, put it in their pocket.[3]

This is also what Mary Douglas has in mind in her ground-breaking anthropological work on the subject when she compares jokes with rites.[4] A rite is here understood as a symbolic act that derives its meaning from a cluster of socially legitimated symbols, such as a funeral. But insofar as the joke plays with the symbolic forms of society – the bishop gets stuck in a lift, I spread margarine on the communion wafer – jokes are *anti-rites*. They mock, parody or deride the ritual practices of a given society, as Milan Kundera remarks, 'Someone's hat falls on the coffin in a freshly dug grave, the funeral loses its meaning and laughter is born'.[5]

Suppose that someone starts to tell you a joke: 'I never left the house as a child. My family were so poor that my mother couldn't afford to buy us clothes'. First, I recognize that a joke is being told and I assent to having my attention caught in this way. Assenting to having my attention caught is very important and if someone interrupts the joke-teller or simply walks away in the middle of the joke, then the tacit social contract of humour has been broken. This is bad form or simply bad manners. Instead of throwing the ball back, I put it in my pocket. In thus assenting and going along with the joke, a certain tension is created in the listener and I follow along willingly with the story that is being recounted. When the punch-line kicks in, and the little bubble of tension pops, I experience an affect that can be described as pleasure, and I laugh or just smile: 'When I was ten, my mother bought me a hat so that I could look out of the window'.

What happens here is, as Kant puts it in a brilliant short discussion of laughter from *The Critique of Judgement*, a sudden evaporation of expectation to nothing ('ein Affekt aus der plötzlichen Verwandlung einer gespannten Erwartung in nichts').[6] In hearing the punch-line, the tension disappears and we experience comic relief. Rather than the tiresome and indeed racist examples of jokes that Kant recounts, involving Indians and bottles of beer, witness Philip Larkin (that celebrated anti-racist!) in a characteristic flourish,

> When I drop four cubes of ice
> Chimingly in a glass, and add
> Three goes of gin, a lemon slice,
> And let a ten-ounce tonic void
> In foaming gulps until it smothers
> Everything else up to the edge,
> I lift the lot in silent pledge:
> *He devoted his life to others.*[7]

The admittedly rather dry humour here is found in a combination of two features: conceptual and rhetorical. On the one hand, there is the conceptual disjunction between the wanton hedonism involved in preparing the gin and tonic, and the avowed altruism of the final line. But also – more importantly – there is the rhetorical effect generated by the sudden bathos of the final line in comparison to the cumulative and almost Miltonic overkill of what precedes it. Picking up on Hobbes's word, it is important to emphasize the necessary *suddenness* of the conceptual and rhetorical shift. Both brevity and speed are the soul of wit.

COMIC TIMING

Mention of the suddenness of the bathetic shift that produces humour brings attention to the peculiar *temporal* dimension of jokes. As any comedian will readily admit, timing is everything, and a mastery of comic forms involves a careful control of pauses, hesitations and silences, of knowing exactly when to detonate the little dynamite of the joke. In this sense, jokes involve a shared knowledge of two temporal dimensions: *duration* and the *instant*. What I mean is that when we give ourselves up to being told a joke, we undergo a peculiar and quite deliberate distention of time, where the practice of joking often involves cumulative repetition and wonderfully needless circumlocution. This is a technique brought to its digressive nadir in the 'shaggy dog' or 'cock and bull' story, such as *Tristram Shandy*.

> Digressions, incontestably, are the sun-shine – they are the life, the soul of reading, – take them out of this book for instance, – you might as well take the book along with them.[8]

In being told a joke, we undergo a particular experience of duration through repetition and digression, of time literally being stretched out like an elastic band. We know that the elastic will snap, we just do not know when, and we find that anticipation rather pleasurable. It snaps with the punch-line, which is a sudden acceleration of time, where the digressive stretching of the joke suddenly contracts into a heightened experience of the instant. We laugh. Viewed temporally, humorous pleasure would seem to be produced by the disjunction between duration and the instant, where we experience with renewed intensity both the slow passing of time and its sheer evanescence.

LAUGHTER AS AN EXPLOSION EXPRESSED WITH THE BODY

It is important to recall that the succession of tension by relief in humour is an essentially bodily affair. That is, the joke invites a corporeal response, from a chuckle, through a giggle to a guffaw. Laughter is a muscular phenomenon, consisting of spasmodic contraction and relaxation of the facial muscles with corresponding movements in the diaphragm. The associated contractions of the larynx and epiglottis interrupt the pattern of breathing and emit sound. Descartes puts the point much more exotically and powerfully in Article 124 of *The Passions of the Soul*,

> Laughter consists in the fact that the blood, which proceeds from the right orifice in the heart by the arterial vein, inflating the lungs suddenly and repeatedly, causes the air which they contain to be constrained and to pass out from them with an impetus by the windpipe, where it forms an inarticulate and explosive utterance; and the lungs in expanding equally with the air as it rushes out, set in motion all the muscles of the diaphragm from the chest to the neck, by which means they cause motion in the facial muscles, which have a certain connection with them. And it is just this action of the face with this inarticulate and explosive voice that we call laughter.

It is just this interruption of breath that distinguishes laughter from smiling, a revealing distinction which will be important for my sense of humour in the conclusion to this book (when all is said and done, it is the smile that interests me most). As a bodily phenomenon, laughter invites comparison with similar convulsive phenomena like orgasm and weeping. Indeed, like the latter, laughter is distinguished by what Helmuth Plessner calls 'A loss of self-control as the break between the person and their body' ('Verlust der Selbstbeherrschung als Bruch zwischen der Person und ihrem Körper').[9] In laughing violently, I lose self-control in a way that is akin to the moments of radical corporeal exposure that follow an orgasm or when crying turns into an uncontrollable sobbing.

Picking up on a word employed by Descartes, and used by a whole tradition extending to Charles Baudelaire, André Breton and Plessner, laughter is an *explosion* expressed with the body. In a lovely formulation, Kant speaks of 'die Schwingung der Organen', 'The oscillation of the organs'. When I laugh vigorously, I literally experience an oscillation or vibration of the organs, which is why it can hurt when you laugh, if you engage in it a little too enthusiastically. Of course, as Jacques Le Goff reminds us, the historical associations between laughter and the body cannot be overemphasized.[10] It is this link to the body that was the reason for the Christian condemnation of laughter in the early Middle Ages, its careful codification in the later Middle Ages, before the explosion of laughter in the early Renaissance, in the work of Rabelais and Erasmus.

CHANGING THE SITUATION

But is that an end to the matter? Hopefully not. For I want to claim that humour is not just comic relief, a transient corporeal affect induced by the raising and extinguishing of tension, of as little social consequence as masturbation, although slightly more acceptable to perform in public. I rather want to claim that what goes on in humour is a form of *liberation* or *elevation* that expresses something essential to what Plessner calls 'the humanity of the human'. We will have to wait until my final chapter, and in particular my use of Freud's conception of humour, before I can make good on this claim. But, as a provisional outline of the thought I am after, let me turn to the character of Eddie Waters, the philosopher-comedian from Trevor Griffiths's brilliant 1976 piece *Comedians*,

> A real comedian – that's a daring man. He *dares* to see what his listeners shy away from, fear to express. And what

he sees is a sort of truth about people, about their situation, about what hurts or terrifies them, about what's hard, above all, about what they *want*. A joke releases the tension, says the unsayable, any joke pretty well. But a true joke, a comedian's joke, has to do more than release tension, it has to *liberate* the will and the desire, it has to *change the situation*.[11]

A true joke, a comedian's joke, suddenly and explosively lets us see the familiar defamiliarized, the ordinary made extra-ordinary and the real rendered surreal, and we laugh in a physiological squeal of transient delight, like an infant playing peek-a-boo: nurse to uncooperative patient, 'We have to see if you have a temperature'; uncooperative patient to nurse, 'Don't be silly, *everybody* has a temperature'. Humour brings about a change of situation, a *surrealization* of the real which is why someone like the great surrealist André Breton was so interested in humour, in particular the unsentimental subversions of what he baptized 'l'humour noir'.[12]

This idea of a change of situation can be caught in Mary Douglas's claim that, 'A joke is a play upon form that affords an opportunity for realising that an accepted pattern has no necessity'.[13] Thus, jokes are a play upon form, where what is played with are the accepted practices of a given society. The incongruities of humour both speak out of a massive congruence between joke structure and social structure, and speak against those structures by showing that they have no necessity. The anti-rite of the joke shows the sheer contingency or arbitrariness of the social rites in which we engage. By producing a consciousness of contingency, humour can change the situation in which we find ourselves, and can even have a *critical* function with respect to society. Hence the great importance that humour has played in social movements that have set out to criticize the established order, such as radical feminist humour: 'How many men does it take to tile a bathroom?', 'I don't know', 'It depends how thinly you slice them'. As the Italian Situationist street slogan has it, 'Una risata vi seppellirà', it will be a laugh that buries you, where the 'you' refers to those in power. By laughing at power, we expose its contingency, we realize that what appeared to be fixed and oppressive is in fact the emperor's new clothes, and just the sort of thing that should be mocked and ridiculed.

REACTIONARY HUMOUR

But before we get carried away, it is important to recognize that not all humour is of this type, and most of the best jokes are fairly reactionary or, at best, simply serve to reinforce social consensus. You will have noticed a couple of paragraphs back that, following Eddie Waters, I introduced the adjective 'true' into our discussion of humour. 'True' humour changes the situation, tells us something about who we are and the sort of place we live in, and perhaps indicates to us how it might be changed. This sounds very nice, but it presupposes a great deal. A number of items cry out for recognition here, some of which will be picked up in later chapters.

Most humour, in particular the comedy of recognition – and most humour is comedy of recognition – simply seeks to reinforce consensus and in no way seeks to criticize the established order or change the situation in which we find ourselves. Such humour does not seek to change the situation, but simply toys with existing social hierarchies in a charming but quite benign fashion, as in P. G. Wodehouse's *The World of Jeeves*. This is the comic as sheer pleasing diversion, and it has an important place in any taxonomy of humour. More egregiously, much humour seeks to confirm the status quo either by denigrating a certain sector of society, as in sexist humour, or by laughing at the alleged stupidity of a social outsider. Thus, the British laugh at the Irish, the Canadians laugh at the Newfies, the Americans laugh at the Poles, the Swedes laugh at the Finns, the Germans laugh at the Ostfrieslanders, the Greeks laugh at the Pontians, the Czechs laugh at the Slovaks, the Russians laugh at the Ukrainians, the French laugh at the Belgians, the Dutch also laugh at the Belgians, and so on and so forth. Such comic scapegoating corresponds to what Hobbes means in suggesting that laughter is a feeling of sudden glory where I find another person ridiculous and laugh at their expense. Such humour is not laughter at power, but the powerful laughing at the powerless.

The reactionary quality of much humour, in particular ethnic humour, must be analysed, which I will attempt in Chapter 4, where I claim that such humour lets us reflect upon the anxious nature of our thrownness in the world. What I mean by the latter is that in its 'untruth', as it were, reactionary humour tells us important truths about who we are. Jokes can therefore be read as symptoms of societal repression and their study might be said to amount to a return of the repressed. In other words, humour can reveal us to be persons that, frankly, we would really rather not be.

STRUCTURED FUN

Humour is being employed as a management tool by consultants – imagine, if you will, a company called 'Humour Solutions International' – who endeavour to show how it can produce greater cohesion amongst the workforce and thereby increase efficiency and productivity. This is beautifully caught in the slogan: 'laughter loves company and companies love laughter'. Some management consultants refer to such activity as 'structured fun', which includes innovations like 'inside out day', where all employees are asked to wear their clothes inside out, or 'silly hat day', which rather speaks for itself. Despite the backslapping bonhomie that such fun must inspire, it is difficult not to feel a little cynical about these endeavours, and the question that one wants to pose to the idea of 'structured fun' is: who is structuring the fun and for what end? Such enforced fun is a form of compulsory happiness, and it is tempting to see it as one further sign of the ways in which employees' private lives are being increasingly regulated by the interests of their employers.

I was recently in Atlanta, staying at a huge hotel, and had occasion to observe some structured fun from my breakfast table one morning. In one of the vast, anonymous, carpeted, windowless suites that pepper every large hotel in the USA, about fifty people from the same company were engaged in collective hopscotch, frisbee and kickball. It was quite a sight and much yelping and clapping was to be heard – the very soundtrack to happiness, I pondered. But looking at the sweating, slightly desperate faces of these mostly overweight grown-ups, one almost felt moved to tears. After breakfast, I found a huddle of employees standing outside, resolutely smoking in the Georgian January drizzle and we exchanged a few words. I was enormously reassured that they felt just as cynical about the whole business as I did, but one of them said that they did not want to appear to be a bad sport or a party pooper at work and that was why they went along with it. Also, he concluded, they were not really offered a choice. I think this incident is interesting for it reveals a vitally subversive feature of humour in the workplace. Namely, that as much as management consultants might try and formalize fun for the benefit of the company, where the comic punch-line and the economic bottom line might be seen to blend, such fun is always capable of being ridiculed by informal, unofficial relations amongst employees, by backchat and salacious gossip. Anyone who has worked in a factory or office knows how the most scurrilous and usually obscene stories, songs and cartoons about the management are the very bread and butter of survival. Humour might well be a management tool but it is also a tool against the management.[14]

JOKES: GOOD, BAD AND GULLIVER

To talk, as I do, of true humour must presuppose some sort of normative claim, namely a distinction between 'good' and 'bad' jokes. However, such a claim must not be reduced to moral crispbread, but must be properly leavened and smeared with tasty examples. I will try and do this below when I make the distinction between *laughing at oneself* and *laughing at others*. In my view, true humour does not wound a specific victim and always contains self-mockery. The object of laughter is the subject who laughs. By way of preparation for this thought, we might cite a few of the closing lines from 'Verses on the Death of Dr Swift', an exquisitely bleak *apologia pro sua vita*,

> Perhaps I may allow the Dean
> Had too much satire in his vein;
> And seemed determined not to starve it,
> Because no age could more deserve it.
> Yet malice never was his aim;
> He lashed the vice but spared the name.
> No individual could resent,
> Where thousands equally were meant.
> His satire points at no defect,

But what all mortals may correct;
For he abhorred that senseless tribe,
Who call it humour when they jibe:
He spar'd a hump or crooked nose,
Whose owners set not up for beaux.
True genuine dullness moved his pity,
Unless it offered to be witty.[15]

The critical task of humour, then, would not be sheer malice or jibing, but the lashing of vices which are general and not personal, 'no individual could resent,/Where thousands equally were meant'. Also, such lashing of vices does not point at a fundamental defect, 'But what all mortals may correct'. That is, true humour can be said to have a therapeutic as well as a critical function. The studied reversals of perspective and fantastical geographical displacements of Swift's *Gulliver's Travels* offer, it is true, a devastating critique of the follies and vices of the modern European world, but the intent of the satire is therapeutic, to bring human beings back from what they have become to what they might be. Satire is often a question of scale, of the familiar becoming infinitely small or grotesquely huge, which can be seen in Gulliver's voyages from the littleness of Lilliput to the bigness of Brobdingnag. But, I would insist, from the studied savaging of modern mathematics, science and government in Laputa and the Academy of Lagado, through to the final descent into misanthropy caused by life with the fully rational animals of the land of the Houyhnhnms, Swift is offering a teaching of virtue that permits Gulliver and the rest of us to be reconciled to life amongst the vicious Yahoos. In my view, this is what Swift means when he complains to Alexander Pope in correspondence from 1725, 'I tell you after all that I do not hate mankind, it is *vous autres* who hate them because you would have them reasonable animals, and are angry for being disappointed'.[16] For, after all, I am a Yahoo and you are too.

LAUGHTER'S MESSIANIC POWER

As well as being something of a revenge of the eighteenth century against the present, in this book I want to defend a two-fold claim: (i) that the tiny explosions of humour that we call jokes return us to a common, familiar world of shared practices, the background meanings implicit in a culture; and (ii) indicate how those practices might be transformed or perfected, how things might be otherwise. Humour both reveals the situation, and indicates how that situation might be changed. That is to say, laughter has a certain redemptive or messianic power. So, does this mean that true humour has to be religious?

The argumentation linking humour to religion is impeccable enough and much great comic writing is Christian, particularly when one thinks of Pope, Swift and Sterne. The briefest glance at M. A. Screech's *Laughter at the Foot of the Cross* confirms the place of laughter in the Bible and in the self-understanding of Christianity through the ages.[17] From the standpoint of the worldly-wise, Christ appears to be a kind of madman. Where the world admires money, power and success, the Christian indifference to these values turns the secular world upside down. It is this folly of the cross that Erasmus understood so well, and which makes his *Praise of Folly* a powerful work of both comedy and confession. Christianity offers us a topsy-turvy world that inverts our worldly values. W. H. Auden is therefore quite right when he says that,

> The world of Laughter is much more closely related to the world of Prayer than either is to the everyday secular world

of Work, for both are worlds in which we are all equal, in the first as individual members of our species, in the latter as unique persons. [. . .] In the world of Work, on the other hand, we are not and cannot be equal, only diverse and interdependent . . . those who try to live by Work alone, without Laughter or Prayer turn into insane lovers of power, tyrants who would enslave Nature to their immediate desires – an attempt which can only end in utter catastrophe, shipwreck on the isle of Sirens.[18]

If laughter lets us see the folly of the world in order to imagine a better world in its place, and to change the situation in which we find ourselves, then I have no objection to the religious interpretation of humour. True jokes would therefore be like shared prayers.

My quibble is rather the following: that the religious world-view invites us to look away from this world towards another in which, in Peter Berger's words, 'the limitations of the human condition are miraculously overcome'.[19] Humour lets us view the folly of the world by affording us the glimpse of another world, by offering what Berger calls 'a signal of transcendence'. However, in my view, humour does not redeem us from this world, but returns us to it ineluctably by showing that there is no alternative. The consolations of humour come from acknowledging that this is the only world and, imperfect as it is and we are, it is only here that we can make a difference. Therefore, the redemptive power of humour is not, as it is in Kierkegaard, the transition from the ethical to the religious point of view, where humour is the last stage of existential awareness before faith. Humour is not nuomenal but phe-nomenal, not theological but anthropological, not numinous but simply luminous. By showing us the folly of the world, humour does not *save* us from that folly by turning our attention elsewhere, as it does in great Christian humour like Erasmus, but calls on us to face the folly of the world and change the situation in which we find ourselves.

SENSUS AND *DISSENSUS COMMUNIS*

Laughter is contagious – think of the intersubjectivity of giggling, particularly when it concerns something obscene in a context where one should be serious, such as listening to a formal academic paper. In such cases, and I am sure (or hope) that we all know them, the laughter can really hurt. One might say that the simple telling of a joke recalls us to what is shared in our everyday practices. It makes explicit the enormous commonality that is implicit in our social life. As we will see in more detail in Chapter 5, this is what Shaftesbury had in mind in the early eighteenth century when he spoke of humour as a form of *sensus communis*. So, humour reveals the depth of what we share. But, crucially, it does this not through the clumsiness of a theoretical description, but more quietly, practically and discreetly. Laughter suddenly breaks out in a bus queue, watching a party political broadcast in a pub, or when someone farts in a lift. Humour is an exemplary practice because it is a universal human activity that invites us to become philosophical spectators upon our lives. It is practically enacted theory. I think this is why Wittgenstein once said that he could imagine a book of philosophy that would be written entirely in the form of jokes.

The extraordinary thing about humour is that it returns us to common sense; by distancing us from it, humour familiarizes us with a common world through its miniature strategies of defamiliarization. If humour recalls us to *sensus communis*, then it does this by momentarily pulling us out of common sense, where jokes function as moments of *dissensus communis*. At its most powerful, say in those insanely punning dialogues between Chico and Groucho Marx, humour is a paradoxical form of speech and action that defeats our expectations, producing laughter with its unexpected verbal inversions, contortions and explosions, a refusal of everyday speech that lights up the everyday, showing it, in Adorno's words, 'as it will one day appear in the messianic light'.[20] Some sundry examples:

1 'What'll I say?', 'Tell them you're not here', 'Suppose they don't believe me?', 'They'll believe you when you start talking'.
2 'Do you believe in the life to come?', 'Mine was always that'.
3 'Have you lived in Blackpool all your life?', 'Not yet'.
4 'Do me a favour and close the window, it's cold outside'. 'And if I close it, will that make it warm outside?'.
5 'Do you want to use a pen?', 'I can't write', 'That's OK, there wasn't any ink in it anyway'.
6 'Which of the following is the odd one out? Greed, envy, malice, anger and kindness'. (*Pause*) 'And'.
7 'Gentlemen, Chicolini here may talk like an idiot, and look like an idiot, but don't let that fool you. He really is an idiot. I implore you, send him back to his father and brothers who are waiting for him with open arms at the penitentiary. I suggest that we give him ten years at Leavenworth, or eleven years at Twelveworth'. 'I tell you what I'll do. I'll take five and ten at Woolworth'.[21]

TRISTRAM SHANDY, OR BACK TO THE THINGS THEMSELVES

To put it in a rather baroque formulation, humour changes the situation in which we find ourselves, or lights up the everyday by providing an 'oblique phenomenology of ordinary life'. The meaning of this claim will hopefully emerge as we proceed, but let me begin to illustrate it by recalling my epigraph from Epictetus, which itself provides the motto to Volumes 1 and 2 of Sterne's *Tristram Shandy*: 'Human beings are troubled with the opinions (*dogmata*) they have of things, and not by the things themselves (*pragmata*).' How is one to understand this epigraph in relation to Sterne's book? Tristram Shandy can evidently be viewed as an extended exploration of the fact that human beings are more troubled with *dogmata*, or their *hobby horses*, than with the things themselves. What Sterne calls 'the Shandian system' is entirely made up of digressions. For example, the digressions on the character and opinions of Mr Walter Shandy show him unable to view the world except through what Sterne calls his *hypotheses*: on names, on noses, on the best technique for birth in order to protect the delicate web of the cerebellum, and so on, and on, and on. And sweet Uncle Toby only sees things hobby-horsically through his obsession with the science of fortification and the attempt to reconstruct the precise dimensions of the siege of Namur where he received the terrible, but ever-obscure, blow to his groin.

Of course, the world viewed from a hobby-horsical, dogmatic perspective inevitably goes awry: Walter Shandy's son is given the wrong name, Tristram instead of Trismegistus, his nose is crushed following a forceps delivery, and the web of the cerebellum – seat of all wisdom – is irreparably crushed following a head-first birth. And I almost forgot to add that Tristram is inadvertently circumcised by a window sash. Uncle

Toby exchanges his heroic campaigns with Corporal Trim on the bowling green for his *amours* with the Widow Wadman, which end in disenchantment when the good Corporal explains to Toby that Mrs Wadman's interest in the wound upon his groin is not simply born from compassion. As Sterne remarks, 'Endless is the quest for truth'.

Yet, where do all these digressions lead? What cosmic truth does the Shandian system reveal to us? Perhaps this: that through the meandering circumlocutions of *Tristram Shandy*, the story of 'a COCK and a BULL . . . and one of the best of its kind, I ever heard', we progressively approach the things themselves, the various *pragmata* that make up the stuff of what we call the ordinary life. That is to say, the infinitely digressive movement of Sterne's prose actually contains a contrary motion within it, which is progressive. We might think of this as a comic phenomenology which is animated by a concern for the things themselves, the things which show themselves when we get rid of our troubling opinions. Humourless dogmatism is replaced by humorous pragmatism. Although it is hardly a Cartesian discourse on the method, Sterne writes of his procedure in the book,

> For in this long digression which I was accidentally led into, as in all my digressions (one only excepted) there is a master-stroke of digressive skill, the merit of which has all along, I fear, been overlooked by my reader, – not for want of penetration in him – but because 'tis an excellence seldom looked for, or expected indeed, in a digression; – and that I fly off from what I am about, as far and as often as any writer in *Great Britain*; yet I constantly take care to order affairs so, that my main business does not stand still in my absence (. . .)

> By this contrivance the machinery of my work is of a
> species by itself; two contrary motions are introduced into it,
> and reconciled, which were thought to be at variance with
> each other. In a word, my work is digressive, and it is
> progressive too, – and at the same time.[22]

This is why, to recall my earlier citation from Sterne, digressions are the sunshine, the life and the soul of reading, 'take them out of this book for instance, – and you might as well take the book along with them'. Inasmuch as the book digresses, it also progresses by a contrary motion. In my view, it is this combination of these two contrary motions – progressive and digressive – that is at the heart of humour. That is to say, through the endless displacement of seeing the world through another's hobby horse, through the eyes of a Walter or a Toby Shandy, one is brought closer to the things themselves, to the finally laughable enigma of ordinary life.

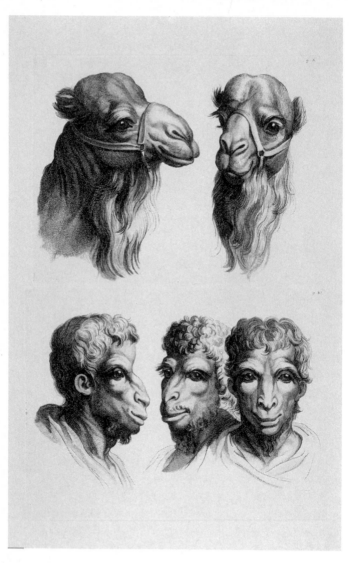

Two heads of a camel and three heads of men in relation to the camel
Source: Cnac-Mnam/Dist RMN. Charles Le Brun

Two

Animals come when their names are called. Just like human beings.

Wittgenstein

Humour is human. Why? Well, because the philosopher, Aristotle, says so. In *On the Parts of the Animals*, he writes, 'no animal laughs save Man'.[1] This quotation echoes down the centuries from Galen and Porphyry, through Rabelais to Hazlitt and Bergson. Now, if laughter is proper to the human being, then the human being who does not laugh invites the charge of inhumanity, or at least makes us somewhat suspicious. Apparently Pythagoras and Anaxagoras never laughed, neither did the Virgin Mary, and Socrates laughed rarely. If laughter is essentially human, then the question of whether Jesus laughed assumes rather obvious theological pertinence to the doctrine of incarnation. One of Beckett's more monstrous anti-heroes, Moran, debates the point with one Father Ambrose,

> Like Job haha, he said. I too said haha. What a joy it is to laugh, from time to time, he said. Is it not? I said. It is peculiar to man, he said. So I have noticed, I said. A brief silence ensued (. . .) Animals never laugh, he said. It takes us to find that funny, I said. What? he said. It takes us to find that funny, I said loudly. He mused. Christ never laughed either, he said, so far as we know. He looked at me. Can you wonder? I said.[2]

As M. A. Screech shows in impressive detail, the theological importance of showing Christ's humanity, and therefore his sense of humour, led many medieval scholars to trawl the Evangelists for evidence of levity.[3] Some support for the case can be found in the first of Christ's recorded miracles, the marriage at Cana (John 2: 1–11). Discovering that the wine has run out, the distraught host somehow alerts Mary, who orders her son to do something about the problem, presumably knowing that he can. This is in itself interesting, as there is no evidence heretofore that Mary was aware that her Son could perform such impressive party tricks. She says to him, 'They have no more wine'; to which Jesus replies somewhat coldly, from his full messianic height, 'Woman, my time has not yet come'. However, like the good Jewish mother who knows what is best for her-Son-the-Messiah, Mary turns to the servants and says 'Do whatever he tells you'. At which point, the water is miraculously turned into wine and the party can continue.

This is an odd moment, bearing a family resemblance to a scene from Monty Python's *The Life of Brian*, where Brian's mother insists, 'He's not the Messiah, he's just a very naughty boy'. Although the joke is on Jesus to some extent insofar as he is made to look slightly foolish by his mother, the marriage at Cana might nonetheless be seen as evidence of humorous humanity on Christ's part. It might indeed appear curious that Jesus' ministry begins with an encouragement to imbibe. However, to the perfervid imagination of medieval Christendom, this first miracle was seen analogically as a New Testament response and recompense for the Old Testament tale of the drunkenness of Noah (Genesis 9: 20–29). Noah was, of course, the first human being to cultivate the vine and sample its fruits, 'and he drank of the wine, and was drunken'. Noah's son, Ham, looked on his inebriated father 'uncovered within his tent' and told his two brothers who walked in backwards and covered his nakedness with a garment. A presumably rather hung-over Noah was none too pleased with Ham and lay an awful curse of servitude on him and all of his Canaanite progeny. Hence the Old and New Testament stories are connected both by theme – wine – and location – Cana. Now, was Ham's sin that of laughter? The Bible does not say.

ECCENTRIC HUMANS

Any philosophical and theological assurance that laughter is unique to the human being becomes somewhat unsure when one turns to the anthropological literature. One need only observe the behaviour of chimpanzees and dogs to see that animals certainly *play*, and they do get frisky, but the question is: do they laugh? They certainly do not seem to laugh at my jokes. But in her 1971 paper, 'Do Dogs Laugh?', Mary Douglas sets out to trouble the assumption that we can divide human from animal along the faultline of laughter.[4] She cites Konrad Lorenz's *Man Meets Dog* and Thomas Mann's *A Man and His Dog* to show how the panting, slightly opened jaws of man's best friend look 'like a human smile' and can give 'a stronger impression of laughing'. However, the evidence is anecdotal and, to my mind, not particularly convincing. The interpretation of the dog's laughter seems rather anthropomorphic and evidence of a crude learnt response on the dog's part, particularly when Lorenz admits that the same facial expression of the dog that denotes 'laughter' also indicates the beginning of erotic excitement, or getting frisky in another way.

We are not going to be able to decide the issue here, and animals are full of surprises. So whilst we cannot say with any certainty whether dogs laugh or not, we can, I think, grant that humour is an anthropological constant, is universal and common to all cultures. There has been no society thus far discovered that did not have humour, whether it is expressed as convulsive, bodily gaiety or with a laconic smile. Thus, humour is a key element in the distinction of the human from the animal; it is a consequence of culture, and indeed of civilization as Cicero's Latin word for humour, *urbanitas*, would suggest. If, as ethologists report, laughter originated in the animal function of the aggressive baring of teeth, then the transformation of the social meaning of this physiological act is one testament to the distance of human culture from animal life.

As Plessner puts it, laughter confirms the eccentric (*exzentrisch*) position of the human being in the world of nature. Plessner's thesis is that the life of animals is *zentrisch*, it is centred. This means that the animal simply lives and experiences (*lebt und erlebt*). By contrast, the human being not only lives and experiences, he or she experiences those experiences (*erlebt sein Erleben*). That is, the human being has a reflective attitude towards its experiences and towards itself. This is why humans are eccentric, because they live beyond the limits set for them by nature by taking up a distance from their immediate experience. In living outside themselves, the reflective activity of human beings achieves a break with nature. Indeed, Plessner goes further and claims that the human is this break, this hiatus, this gap between the physical and the psychical. The working out of the consequences of the eccentric position of the human is the main task of a philosophical anthropology, which is why laughter has such an absolutely central role in Plessner's work.[5]

Plessner's thesis is pretty convincing, but is it true to say that animals always exist in sheer immediacy? Do they – even the cleverest of them – always fail to take up an eccentric position with regard to their life, not even when they seem to know that they are going to die? In a word, are all animals incapable of reflection? I simply do not know, and if a lion could talk then we could not understand him. Furthermore, I do not know how Plessner can know what he seems so sure of, namely that animals are incapable of reflection. Let us just say that I have my doubts about Plessner's certitude.

A SMALL BESTIARY

If humour is human, then it also, curiously, marks the limit of the human. Or, better, humour explores what it means to be human by moving back and forth across the frontier that separates humanity from animality, thereby making it unstable, and troubling the hiatus of which Plessner speaks. Humour is precisely the exploration of the break between nature and culture, which reveals the human to be not so much a category by itself as a negotiation between categories. We might even define the human as a *dynamic* process produced by a series of identifications and misidentifications with animality.[6] Thus, what makes us laugh is the reduction of the human to the animal or the elevation of the animal to the human. The fact that we label certain comic genres in animalistic terms, like 'Cock and Bull' or 'shaggy dog' stories is perhaps revealing.

Examples of bestiality in literature are legion, from Aesop's fables, through to Chaucer's Chaunticleer in *The Nun's Priest's Tale* and *Le Roman de Renard*. Animals litter the history of literature, in particular parrots, dogs, cats and bears. A more bizarre example of the identification with animality, because of the unhappy mental state of the author and the fact that it was penned in Mr Potter's mad house in Bethnal Green, is

Christopher Smart's *Jubilate Agno* written sometime between 1758 and 1763. Smart begins thus,

> For I will consider my Cat Jeoffry.
> For he is the servant of the Living God duly and daily serving him
> For at the first glance of the glory of God in the East he worships in his way.
> For is this done by wreathing his body seven times round with elegant quickness.

And so on, and so forth, for page after rambling page. My favourite lines are the following,

> For by stroking him I have found out electricity.
> For I perceived God's light about him both wax and fire.
> For the Electrical fire is the spiritual substance, which God sends from heaven to sustain the bodies of both man and beast.
> For God has blest him in the variety of his movements.
> For tho' he cannot fly, he is an excellent clamberer.
> For his motions upon the face of the earth are more than any other quadrupede.
> For he can tread to all the measures upon the music.
> For he can swim for life.
> For he can creep.[7]

Smart was sadly less than smart when he wrote these lines, but their electrical warmth expresses something approaching humanity towards Jeoffry the cat.

The exploration of the hiatus between the human and the animal is obviously at the heart of Book IV of *Gulliver's Travels*, where the power of Gulliver's identification with the rational animals or Houyhnhnms is proportionate to his misanthropic disgust at his all-too-human Yahoo-ness. Swift explores a similar paradox in 'The Beast's Confession to the Priest' by way of a critique of Aesop's 'libelling of the four-foot race',

> For, here he owns, that now and then
> Beasts may degenerate into men.[8]

This comic inversion of the human and the animal continues in the twentieth century in Orwell's *Animal Farm* and Kafka's *Metamorphosis*, a text that Breton quite properly places in his *Anthologie de l'humour noir*, but he might also have included many of Kafka's ever-strange short stories, such as 'Investigations of a Dog' and 'Josephine the Singer, or the Mouse-Folk'. This tradition continues on to a book like Will Self's *Great Apes*, not to mention a whole tradition of satirical cartooning whose contemporary expression would be Gary Larson's *The Far Side*.

HORACE AND JUVENAL, URBANITY AND DISGUST

The two effects produced by such humour here might be considered in terms of the distinction between the benign mockery or *urbanitas* of Horatian satire, and the brooding, black misanthropy of Juvenalian satire. In the eighteenth century, of course, this is the distinction between the satires of Pope and Swift and the accompanying genres of mock-heroic and travesty: the epic elevation of the insignificant and the deflationary belittling of the sublime. On the one hand we find the comic urbanity of the animal, where the humour is generated by the sudden and incongruous humanity of the animal. A wonderful example of this is given by Peter Berger,

A bear is charging this hunter in the woods. The hunter fires, and misses. The bear breaks his rifle in two, sodomizes the hunter, then walks away. The hunter is furious. The next day he is back in the woods, with a new rifle. Again the bear charges, again the hunter misses, again he is sodomized. The hunter is now beside himself. He is going to get that bear, if it's the last thing he does. He gets himself an AK-47 assault rifle, goes back into the woods. Again the bear charges and, believe it or not, again the hunter misses. The bear breaks the assault rifle, gently puts his paws around the hunter and says, 'OK, come clean now. This isn't really about hunting, is it?'[9]

On the other hand, the Juvenalian reduction of the human to the animal does not so much produce mirth as a comic disgust with the species. This is something which Petronius employs to great effect in 'Trimalchio's Feast' from the *Satyricon*, where the slave Trimalchio – himself some sort of twisted reflection of Petronius's employer, the Emperor Nero – appears like a great, shining pig. His epitaph, composed himself in what Beckett would call pigsty Latin, reads,

> Here Lies C. Pompeius Trimalchio
> He could have had any job in Rome
> But didn't.
> Loyal, brave and true,
> He started with a nickel in his pocket,
> And left his heirs thirty million;
> AND HE NEVER ONCE LISTENED TO A PHILOSOPHER.[10]

Whether we think of Yahoos shitting from trees, Gregor Samsa wriggling on his back, or Orwell's further twisting of the animal-human coupling by presenting the tyrant Napoleon finally upright on two legs, the history of satire is replete with Juvenalian echoes. In his oddly eighteenth-century novel, *Great Apes*, Will Self writes,

Sarah sat at the bar of the Sealink Club being propositioned by men. Some men propositioned her with their eyes, some with their mouths, some with their heads, some with their hair. Some men propositioned her with nuance, exquisite subtlety; others propositioned her with chutzpah, their suit as obvious as a schlong slammed down on the zinc counter. Some men's propositioning was so slight as to be peripheral, a seductive play of the minor parts, an invitation to touch cuticles, rub corns, hang nails. Other men's propositioning was a Bayreuth production, complete with mechanical effects, great flats descending, garishly depicting their Taste, their Intellect, their Status. The men were like apes – she thought – attempting to impress her by waving and kicking things about in a display of mock potency.[11]

When the animal becomes human, the effect is pleasingly benign and we laugh out loud, 'OK come clean now. This isn't really about hunting, is it?' But when the human becomes animal, the effect is disgusting and if we laugh at all then it is what Beckett calls 'the mirthless laugh', which laughs at that which is unhappy.

Staying with the example of Will Self, it seems to me that he combines both Horatian and Juvenalian effects in a wonderfully macabre short story called 'Flytopia'. One sultry summer, in the somnolent Suffolk village of Inwardleigh, our hero Jonathan is trying to complete the index to a tome on ecclesiastical architecture. Irritated by the insects which plague his cottage and break his concentration, he resolves to destroy them with the use of sundry toxic products. Then awakening one morning, after insect-haunted nightmares, a pullulating mass of silverfish on his draining board shape themselves into the words, 'WELCOME TO FLYTOPIA'. He then enters into a bizarre contract with the insects: they cease bothering him and keep the house clean and he lets them live and even feeds them. The Horatian humour consists in the sometimes protracted dialogues on the draining board with the silverfish, with Jonathan pedantically correcting their spelling. But the effect becomes more Juvenalian when we are treated to the image of Jonathan's person being cleaned by his new-found insect friends, 'He found their assistance in his toilet not simply helpful, but peculiarly sensual'. Finally, after having agreed to give over a spare bedroom to his insects, for breeding and feeding purposes, he happily sacrifices his girlfriend, unhappily called Joy, in response to their request for 'MORE MEAT',

> Jonathan listened to her feet going up the stairs. He listened to the door of the spare bedroom open, he heard the oppressive giant fluttering hum, as she was engulfed, then he rose and went out to pay the cab.[12]

OUTLANDISH ANIMALS

Humour is human. But what makes us laugh is the inversion of the animal-human coupling, whether it is Horatian urbanity or Juvenalian disgust. If being human means being humorous, then being humorous often seems to mean becoming an animal. But, paradoxically, what becoming an animal confirms is the fact that humans are *incapable* of becoming animals. For, the sad truth is that in humour humans show themselves to be useless animals; hopeless, incompetent, outlandish animals, shitting from trees and grunting like great apes. There is something charming about an animal become human, but when the human becomes animal, then the effect is disgusting.

All of which confirms the human being's eccentric position in the world of nature. Consider the following remark from Wittgenstein,

> Two people are laughing together, say at a joke. One of them has used certain somewhat unusual words and now they both break out into a sort of bleating. This might appear *very* extraordinary to a visitor coming from quite a different environment. Whereas we find it quite *reasonable*.
>
> (I recently witnessed this scene on a bus and was able to think myself into the position of the someone to whom this would be unfamiliar. From that point of view, it struck me as quite irrational, like the responses from an outlandish *animal*.)[13]

There is something rather surreal about visualizing Wittgenstein on a double-decker bus thinking that thought whilst watching two people imitating sheep, but that is not the point. Satire works in precisely the way he describes. Namely, we are asked to look at ourselves as if we were visitors from an alien environment, to examine terrestrial existence from a Martian point of view. When we do this, then we begin to look like outlandish animals, and reasonableness crumbles into irrationality. This can be linked to an idea dear to the French philosopher Gilles Deleuze, what he calls 'deterritorialization', and which he interestingly chooses to translate into English as 'outlandishness'.[14] The critical task of the writer is to write from the place of the animal, to look at human affairs with a dog's or beetle's eye, as in Kafka's stories.

Satire transforms us into outlandish animals, and the natural history of humanity is the vast research archive of the writer. By criss-crossing the frontier between the human and the animal, writers like Swift or Kafka produce a kind of shock effect that shakes us up and effects a critical change of perspective. Satire stands resolutely against the self-images of the age. Adorno famously writes that the only thing that is true in psychoanalysis is the exaggerations. But this would seem to be even more true of satire. In Book IV of *Gulliver's Travels*, Swift was not persuaded of the existence of talking horses. Rather, his critical point is that there is nothing to prevent this possibility once we begin to conceive of ourselves as rational animals. The truth of satire is obviously not to be assessed in terms of literal verifiability, but rather to warn us against a danger implicit in our self-conception. To have an effect, the warning signals have to be deafening.

KANT'S PARROT

In this chapter, we have been pursuing an interesting paradox. On the one hand, humour is what picks us out as human, it is what is proper to the human being, situated as we are between beasts and angels. Humour confirms the human being's eccentric position in nature, as improper within it, as reflectively alienated from the physical realm of the body and external nature. Yet, on the other hand, what takes place in humour, particularly in satire, is the constant overstepping of the limit between the human and the animal, demonstrating their uneasy neighbourhood. But, bringing together both sides of this paradox, we might say that the studied incongruities of humour show the eccentric position of the human in nature by recalling the benign humanity of the animal and the disturbing animality of the human. The human being is amphibious, like a boat drawn up on the shore, half in the water, half out of it. We are a paradox.

Mention of water brings to mind a final maritime example of humour, humans and animals in Thomas Bernhard's wonderful 1978 play *Immanuel Kant*. Kant is sailing to America, the country that was always for him 'eine Perversität', to receive an honorary doctorate from Columbia University and to have an operation for his glaucoma. Of course, absolutely none of this is true. Kant travels in the company of Frau Kant, his servant Ernst Ludwig, and his parrot Friedrich. Being Kant's parrot, Friedrich has awesome philosophical ability. Indeed, Kant says that the great Leibniz declined to give a lecture in Königsberg because he knew that Friedrich the parrot would be present. The whole piece has a wonderfully Dadaist, almost dreamlike, quality which is crowned by the mini-dialogues between Kant and his parrot, where the animal bathetically mirrors the great philosopher's words. Let me give a flavour of the German alongside my translation,

Kant:	(*Kant*:
Ich bin von Anfang an	From the beginning
nur mit Friedrich gereist	I only travelled with Friedrich
heimlich	clandestinely
naturgemäß	naturally
durch ganz Deutschland	through all of Germany
Kant ist aus Königsberg	It is said that
nicht hinausgekommen	Kant never
wird gesagt	left Königsberg
aber wo Kant ist	but where Kant is
ist Königsberg	is Königsberg
Königsberg ist	Königsberg is
wo Kant ist	where Kant is
(*zu Friedrich*)	(*to Friedrich*)
Wo ist Königsberg?	Where is Königsberg?
Friedrich:	*Friedrich*:
Wo Kant ist	Where Kant is

Kant:	*Kant*:
Und wo ist Kant?	And where is Kant?
Friedrich:	*Friedrich*:
Kant ist wo Königsberg ist.[15]	Kant is where Königsberg is.)

Much could be said about parrots. They are surely the most unnerving of animals because of their uncanny ability to imitate that which is meant to pick us out as a species: language. Comic echo of the human, holding up a ridiculing mirror to our faces, the parrot is the most critical beast of all the field. The first century Neapolitan poet Statius writes,

> PARROT, Prince among birds, delightful slave,
> you speak just like a person, and make more sense
> than most, repeating to us what we say to you.[16]

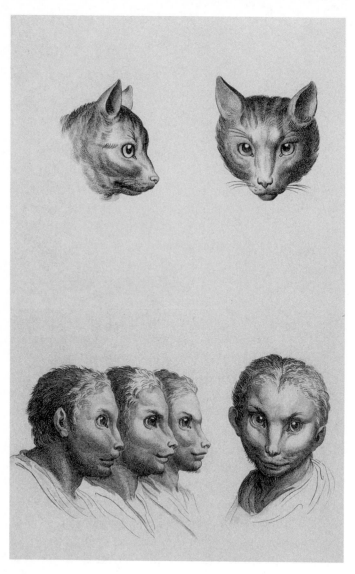

Two heads of a cat and four heads of men in relation to the cat
Source: Cnac-Mnam/Dist RMN. Charles Le Brun

Three

Ich bin, aber ich habe mich nicht
(I am, but I do not have myself)

The incongruities of humour light up the eccentricity of the human situation with regard to ourselves and nature. Humour effects a breakage in the bond connecting the human being to its unreflective, everyday existence. In humour, as in anxiety, the world is made strange and unfamiliar to the touch. When I laugh or just smile, I see myself as the outlandish animal that I am, and begin to reflect on what I had previously taken for granted. In this sense, humour might be said to be one of the conditions for taking up a critical position with respect to what passes for everyday life, producing a change in our situation which is both liberating and elevating, but also *captivating*, showing all too clearly the capture of the human being in the nets of nature. In this sense, we might want to describe our sapience and our humanity as powerfully exemplified in the attainment of a humorous attitude.

Homo sapiens is therefore not so much *homo ludens* as Johan Huizinga famously argued, where humanity would be identified with the capacity to play. Rather, we are *homo ridens*, laughing beings, or indeed, *homo risibilis*, which suggests both 'the risible or ridiculous being', and 'the being gifted with laughter'.[1] Humour is human, all-too-human. In Hebrew, the name 'Isaac' or 'Isha-ak' means 'the one who will laugh', and the fact that, in Genesis 17, God himself chooses this name for the son of ninety-nine-year-old Abram and the ninety-year-old Sarai shows that He too is not without a sense of humour. Indeed, on hearing that a child will be born to him, Abram incredulously falls down laughing. As reward for their faith in Him, God adds syllables to the elderly couple's names, becoming AbrAHam and SarAH – an onomatopoeic 'Ha-Ha'.

BEING AND HAVING

I would now like to focus these thoughts in relation to the body, which is the butt of so much humour. In his very useful study of laughter, Peter Berger recalls Max Scheler's distinction between *being* and *having*.[2] Let us assume, classically enough, that the animal *is* its body. I simply do not know whether this is true (if a lion could speak then we could not understand him, but when a parrot does speak then we assume that he does not understand himself. But who knows?). The claim here is that the eccentric position of the human being in nature is confirmed by the fact that not only *are* we our bodies, we also *have* our bodies. That is, the human being can subjectively distance itself from its body, and assume some sort of critical position with respect to itself. This is most obviously the case in the experience of illness, where one might say that in pain we all try and turn ourselves into Cartesian mind/body dualists. In pain, I attempt to take a distance from my body, externalize the discomfort and insulate myself in thought, something which occurs most obviously when we lie anxiously prone in the dentist's chair. But more generally, there are a whole range of experiences, most disturbingly in anorexia, where the body that I *am* becomes the body that I *have*, the body-*subject* becomes an *object* for me, which confirms both the possibility of taking up a critical position, and also underlines my *alienation* from the world and nature.

Yet, the curious thing about such experiences is that if I can distance myself from my body, where being becomes having and subject becomes object, then can I ever overcome that distance? If, the moment that reflection begins, I become a stranger to myself, a foreign land, then can I simply return home to unreflective familiarity? Might one not conjecture that human beings, as eccentric animals, are defined by this continual failure to coincide with themselves? Does not our identity precisely consist in a lack of self-identity, in the fact that identity is always a question for us – a quest, indeed – that we might vigorously pursue, but it is not something I actually possess? It is this situation that is suggested by my epigraph: I most certainly *am*, but yet I do not *have* myself.

PHYSICS AND METAPHYSICS

This is perhaps a disturbing, perhaps a consoling thought. Let me try and explain how it works in relation to humour. Humour functions by exploiting the gap between being a body and having a body, between – let us say – the *physical* and *metaphysical* aspects of being human. What makes us laugh, I would wager, is the return of the physical into the metaphysical, where the pretended tragical sublimity of the human collapses into a comic ridiculousness which is perhaps even more tragic. *Vene, vidi, vici* says the great Kenneth Williams playing the dying Caesar in what is, for me, the best of the classic British *Carry On* films, 'I came, I saw . . . *(pause, he expires)* . . . I conked out'. We might pause to recall that when Williams took his own life in 1988, his final words were 'Oh, what's the bloody point?'[3] Funny, eh?

Yet, if humour is the return of the physical into the meta-physical, then its physicality is essentially that of the body. The physical particles of the comic universe are the body parts, what Bakhtin rather euphemistically calls 'the material-bodily-lower-stratum'.[4] If we laugh with the body, then what we often laugh at is the body, the strange fact that we *have* a body. In humour, it is as if we temporarily inhabited a Gnostic universe, where the fact of our materiality comes as some-thing of a surprise. This is why the administration of humour is delegated to the Ministry of Silly Walks. One thinks of the way in which certain comics, like John Cleese, so awkwardly inhabit their bodies. Even more powerfully, one thinks of Monsieur Hulot's visible disconnection with his body, exacerbated with its short, ill-fitting raincoat, too-short trousers, and trilby, all of which merely emphasize his strangeness with regard to the world in which he finds himself.

If humour takes place in the gap between being a body and having a body, then Will Self is someone who delights in this gap. His 1992 book, *Cock and Bull*, is made up of two stories: in *Cock*, a woman grows a penis and rapes her useless, ex-alcoholic husband. In *Bull*, a man who grows a vagina behind his knee is seduced by his male doctor. What interests me here is the way in which the protagonists experience this somewhat unexpected transformation. After a slow process of realization, Carol, the heroine in *Cock*, finally realizes what has slowly been taking shape between her legs for the past few weeks,

> Carol stood in front of the full-length mirror that formed the cupboard door, regarding *its* incongruity: peeking out from her hair-bedraggled lips, devoid of the pouch that perhaps ought to accompany it. She sat down on the edge of the bed and the fingers of both her hands toyed with *it*. *It* was at

> least three, or even five centimetres long. A pinky-brown
> roll of flesh could be pulled back from its tip to reveal a
> little mushroom, in the centre of which was a dry eye. It
> was, Carol decided, a penis.[5]

This is pure *having*. The body, which is indeed Carol's own,
albeit customized, is experienced as radically alien, as belong-
ing to another sex. Will Self wonderfully elicits a sort of sensual
disgust, or, better, a disgust produced by an excessively acute
description of the sensuous, where all the awful imperfections
of the flesh are revealed by being too microscopically detailed.
The way such humour works is through a play of distance
and proximity, where the reader has their nose rubbed in the
physical object being described, but in a manner that is remote
and resolutely unsentimental. It is a little like Gulliver's trip
to the giants of Brobdingnag, where he describes in horrible
detail the breast of a female giant,

> It stood prominent six foot and could not be less than
> sixteen in circumference. The nipple was about half the
> bigness of my head, and the hue both of that and the dug so
> varified with spots, pimples and freckles, that nothing could
> appear more nauseous.[6]

In humour, there seems to be an unspoken contract between
misanthropy (and, in Swift's case, misogyny) and sensuality.
The body is comically distanced in being so closely described
and the self wilfully and eccentrically tries to pull out of its
orbit.

OUR SOULS, ARSEHOLES

The comedy of the body is most obviously and crudely
exemplified in scatological humour, where the distinction
between the metaphysical and the physical is explored in the

gap between our souls and arseholes, where we are asked to look at the world with the 'nether eye' that is the focus for the completely anal wit of Chaucer's *The Miller's Tale*.

> This Nicholas anon let flee a fart,
> As greet as it had been a thonder-dent,
> That with the strook he was almost yblent;
> And he was redy with his iren hoot,
> And Nicholas amydde the ers he smoote.[7]

This is the research field that I want to baptize 'post-colonial theory'.[8] Of course, the undisputed heavyweight champion of scatological wit is Rabelais. We find Gargantua injuriously free-associating in the following manner,

> Shittard
> Squittard
> Crackard
> Turduous
> Thy bung
> Has flung
> Some dung
> On us.
> Filthard
> Cackard
> Stinkard
> May you burn with St Anthony's fire
> If all
> Your foul
> Arseholes
> Are not well wiped ere you retire.[9]

Connecting this with what I said above about animality, the body returns in laughter in the form of an eruptive, animal physicality. In this sense, animal jokes are a sort of code for the body and its rather wayward desires – 'look, this isn't really about hunting is it?'

Another splendidly tasteless example of scatological wit is Swift's 'Cassinus and Peter: A Tragical Elegy', which concludes with the unforgettable couplet,

> Nor, wonder how I lost my wits;
> Oh! Celia, Celia, Celia shits.[10]

The joke here is not on Celia, but on Cassinus and Peter, 'Two college sophs of Cambridge growth/Both special wits, and lovers both'. The bathetic final couplet comes at the end of an agonizingly prolix series of circumlocutions where Peter tries to ascertain from Cassinus what it is about Celia, his love, that ails him so. The author being Dean Swift, the humour here is gratuitously direct. What makes us laugh is the return of the most physical of facts into the spiritual seclusion of the two beautiful souls – the return of being into having.

PEDITOLOGY

And whilst we are trying to look at things with 'the nether eye', we should consider the lowly fart, for if the body is what returns in humour then surely the fart is both the auditory and olfactory announcement of the body's imminent return. My favourite example of what might be called *pedito*-logical wit comes from Beckett's *Molloy*, where the eponymous hero engages the topic of the impermeablility of *The Times Literary Supplement*,

Chameleon in spite of himself, there you have Molloy, viewed from a certain angle. And in winter, under my greatcoat, I wrapped myself in swathes of newspaper, and did not shed them until the earth awoke, for good, in April. *The Times Literary Supplement* was admirably adapted to this purpose, of a never failing toughness and impermeability. Even farts made no impression on it. I can't help it, gas escapes from my fundament on the least pretext, it's hard not to mention it now and then, however great my distaste. One day I counted them. Three hundred and fifteen farts in nineteen hours, or an average of over sixteen farts an hour. After all, it's not excessive. Four farts every fifteen minutes. It's nothing. Not even one fart every five minutes. It's unbelievable. Damn it, I hardly fart at all, I should never have mentioned it. Extraordinary how mathematics help you to know yourself.[11]

What is so humorous here is not the simple admission of farting – which is not *that* funny in itself, despite the unforgettably direct farting scene in Mel Brooks' 1974 film *Blazing Saddles* – but the way in which Molloy concocts a mathematical analysis of his flatulence, dividing the 315 farts in something like a travesty of the technique of the division of the theme in a medieval sermon. The tension we feel in reading or listening to this passage is produced by the sheer incongruity between the item under discussion – farting – and the mathematical method for treating it. We are led from one end of the joke to the other with a feeling of increasing absurdity whose conclusion produces a straightforward logical contradiction: having begun by admitting to gas escaping his fundament on the least pretext, Molloy concludes by denying his original statement, 'Damn it, I hardly fart at all'. At this point, the whole scene seems to evaporate into nothing as Kant would put it, to go up in a cloud of rather odious smoke. The realization that our willing suspension of disbelief has simply resulted in an elaborate piece of nonsense, makes us laugh. It is a wonderful example of what Freud means by humour being an economy in the expenditure of affect.

However, that is not the end of the story, for there then follows a typically Beckettian flourish that can be described in terms of what Beckett calls 'the syntax of weakness'. This is a syntax that can be found throughout Beckett's work in a whole series of wonderfully self-undoing, self-weakening phrases: 'Live and invent. I have tried, Invent. It is not the word. Neither is live. No matter. I have tried'.[12] The thought that I would like briefly to follow here is humour as a syntax of weakness, as a comic syntax. To see how this might work, let me go back to the quotation from *Molloy*. I laugh at the phrase, 'Damn it, I hardly fart at all', but then Molloy adds the clause, 'I should never have mentioned it'. I think this has the effect of making the laughter stick in our throats, calling it into question, and acknowledging that perhaps the whole joke was simply a waste of time, a mere bubble. This would seem to be compounded by the final phrase of the passage, 'Extraordinary how mathematics help you to know yourself'. Regardless of how much mathematics might be said to contribute to self-knowledge, it is clear that in the case at hand, it has contributed exactly nothing at all. Mathematics meanders into meaninglessness or at least into the paralysed stoicism described in *Murphy*.

The genius of Beckett's humour is that he makes us laugh and then calls us into question through that laughter. This is the highest laugh, the mirthless laugh, the laugh laughing at the laugh, the *risus purus* of the epigraph to this book. It is laughter that opens us up and causes our defences to drop momentarily, but it is precisely at that moment of weakness that Beckett's humour rebounds upon the subject. We realize in an instant that the object of laughter is the subject who laughs. After the wave of laughter has hit us with its saline spray, an undertow of doubt threatens to drag us under the water's surface. And there is no wave without the undertow.

THE BLACK SUN AT THE CENTRE OF THE COMIC UNIVERSE

Let me go back to the body. If humour is, as I suggested, the return of the physical into the metaphysical, then it is important to point out that the human being remains an ineluctably metaphysical entity, which was what I meant with the amphibious image of the human being as a rowing boat, half in the water, half out of it. If the bodily dimension of the comic takes place in the gap between being and having, between our souls and arseholes, then this hole cannot be plugged or bunged up. We cannot simultaneously *be* what we *have*. The critical distance with regard to the world and nature that opens up in the incongruities of humour is testified to in the alienation we experience with regard to our bodies. This is why the experience of the body in pain is so oddly analogous to the pleasures of laughter – which is why it can hurt when you laugh. As the example from Beckett indicates, when the laughter dies away, we sense, with a sadness – a *Tristram-tristesse* – that is always the dark heart of humour, what an oddity the human being is in the universe. Ultimately, it is this moment when the laughter dies away, the black sun of depression at the centre of the comic universe, that irresistibly attracts me. In humour we orbit eccentrically around a black sun. In Peter Chelsom's wonderful 1994 film *Funny Bones*, one of the legendary Parker Brothers says in his first words in 12 years, 'Nobody's pain is like ours, but the moon's dark side draws the tides'.

To put this in other words, if humour is the return of the physical into the metaphysical, then this does not mean that we can return to the physical. We cannot go back to the position where we *are* our bodies, because we continually stumble over the fact that we *have* them. Such is the curse of reflection. Furthermore, we *have* our bodies in a way that can unsettle the way they *are*, as is revealed in the numerous, multiple conversion hysteria to which we are prone – eczema, acne, rashes, nausea, convulsive vomiting, coughing, tics, etc. In this sense, importantly I think, comic figures like Panurge and Gargantua, or Harlequin and Scaramouche from the *commedia dell'arte*, or even Sir John Falstaff, do not represent *human* possibilities, but rather some outbreak of the inhuman or the more-than-human, some reminder of a relation to the body that is not available to us. *Inter alia*, this is my worry about Mikhail Bakhtin, whose identification of a culture of laughter (*Lachenkultur*) with 'the immortal collective popular body', is both historically questionable, because so much medieval and early renaissance humour was a terribly learned and clerical affair, but can also lead to a romanticization and heroization of the body.[13] In my view, the body that is the object and subject of humour is an *abject* body – estranged, alien, weakening, failing. I think Larkin is once again closer to the truth in his comically cruel description of senescence in 'The Old Fools',

> At death, you break up: the bits that were you
> Start speeding away from each other for ever
> With no one to see. It's only oblivion, true:
> We had it before, but then it was going to end,
> And was all the time merging with a unique endeavour
> To bring to bloom the million-petalled flower
> Of being here. Next time you can't pretend
> There'll be anything else.[14]

There is a metaphysical unease at the heart of humour that turns on the sheer difficulty of making our being coincide with our having of that being. We are eccentric creatures doomed to experience ourselves with what Nietzsche calls a 'pathos of distance' that is both the mark of our nobility and the fact of our solitude, an existential bleakness, a basic ineradicable human loneliness. This is why the highest laughter, the mirthless laughter, sticks in our throats, a little like when we recall Kenneth Williams' desperate final words, or, indeed, when we think of the final words of Bill Beckett, Sam's deeply mourned father, whose final words to his son were 'Fight, fight, fight', followed by 'What a morning'.[15] Funny, eh?

Three heads of an owl and three heads of men in relation to the owl
Source: Cnac-Mnam/Dist RMN. Charles Le Brun

The Laughing Machine – a Note on Bergson and Wyndham Lewis

Four

Eigentlich komisch ist nur der Mensch
(Really, only the human being is comical)

Plessner

Alongside Freud's 1905 *Jokes and Their Relation to the Unconscious*, Henri Bergson's *Le rire* from 1900 is the theory of laughter that exerted the greatest influence in the twentieth century. Bergson's principal thesis is the following,

> Let us then return, for the last time, to our central image: something mechanical encrusted on something living (*du mécanique plaqué sur du vivant*). Here, the living being under discussion was a human being, a person. A mechanical arrangement, on the other hand, is a thing. What, therefore, incited laughter was the momentary transformation of a person into a thing, if one considers the image from this standpoint. Let us then pass from the exact idea of a machine to the vaguer one of a thing in general. We shall have a fresh series of laughable images which will be obtained by taking a blurred impression, so to speak, of the outlines of the former and will bring us to this new law: *we laugh every time a person gives us the impression of being a thing* (*Nous rions toutes les fois qu'une personne nous donne l'impression d'une chose*).[1]

Two claims are being made in this passage: first, that the central image of Bergson's book is the mechanical encrusted onto the living; second, what makes us laugh is a person who gives us the impression of a thing. Bringing together these two claims, we laugh when a human being or another living being, whose behaviour we imagine we can predict, begins to appear somehow thingly or machine-like. Humour therefore consists in the momentary transformation of the physical into the machinic, when the mechanical encrusts itself onto the living like plaque on the surface of a tooth. The comic figure, and Bergson is thinking of characters like Don Quixote and Baron Von Münchhausen, is a person becoming a thing, becoming machine-like, becoming what the French call *machin*, thinga-majig. What fascinates Bergson is the comic quality of the automaton, the world of the jack-in-the-box, the marionette, the doll, the robot.

The two core concepts in Bergson's discussion of laughter are rigidity (*raideur*) and repetition. The comic figure possesses, or better, is possessed by *un effect de raideur*, a certain stiffness or inflexibility which is emphasized through an absent-minded, almost unconscious, mechanical repetitiveness. This is obviously the case in mime and visual humour, but equally in cartoons, where Tom endlessly repeats his pursuit of Jerry, and the Coyote never catches his Road Runner. There is a compulsion to repeat in the comic, a repetitiveness that is also endemic to the machinic, whether one thinks of photo-copiers, soda machines or air-conditioning units. At its humorous edges, the human begins to blur with the machine, becoming an inhuman thing that stands over against the human being. This is why the feeling that often accompanies laughter is not simply pleasure, but rather uncanniness. We often laugh because we are troubled by what we laugh at, because it somehow frightens us. This is particularly the case with gallows humour, as for example in the story that Groucho Marx used to like to relate about a man who was condemned to be hanged. The priest says to him, 'Have you any last words before we spring the trap?' And the condemned man says, 'Yes, I don't think this damn thing is safe'.

Bergson's book was published in 1900, at the dawn of that quintessentially twentieth-century art form: cinema. André Breton notes the early and enduring love affair between cinema and humour, from the early comedies of Mack Sennett, through to Chaplin, Buster Keaton, Harold Lloyd, Laurel and Hardy and the Marx Brothers.

> Cinema was obliged to encounter humour almost straight away because film not only – like poetry – represents the successive situations of life, but also claims to take account of their interconnection and enchainment and in order to affect the emotions of the spectator it is obliged to employ extreme solutions.[2]

Now, in my view, Bergson's account of laughter really comes alive when one thinks of silent cinema. Whether it is the mechanical rigidity of Chaplin's body, the person-become-thing of Keaton's face or the mute perversity of Harpo Marx, humour is here produced by the different ways in which the mechanical or thingly encrusts itself onto the living. In Beckett's 1965 *Film*, a tragically haggard Buster Keaton achieves this effect by staring impassively into the camera. In Chaplin's finally too didactic anti-capitalist parable, *Modern Times*, the little protagonist literally becomes an automaton, submitting himself absent-mindedly to the endless repetitiveness of the industrial production process. Chaplin satirizes the industrial machine by becoming a machine himself, in one memorable scene literally being ingested by the cogs of the industrial leviathan.

A CABBAGE READING FLAUBERT – NOW THAT'S FUNNY

So, let us grant Bergson his thesis: we laugh when a person gives us the impression of a thing, when the mechanical encrusts itself onto the living. But if that is true, then is the opposite thesis also not true? Namely, do we also not laugh when a thing gives us the impression of a person? This is the position argued for by Wyndham Lewis, artist, avant-gardist and creator of Vorticism, who came up with such choice phrases as 'Laughter is the brain-body's snort of exultation'. In a fine brief essay from 1927, 'The Meaning of the Wild Body', Lewis writes against Bergson,

> The root of the Comic is to be sought in the sensations resulting from the observations of a *thing* behaving like a person. But from that point of view all men are necessarily comic: for they are all *things*, or physical bodies, behaving as *persons*. It is only when you come to deny that they are 'persons', or that there is any 'mind' or 'person' there at all, that the world of appearance is accepted as quite natural, and not at all ridiculous. Then, with a denial of 'the person', life becomes immediately both 'real' and very serious.
>
> To bring vividly to our mind what we mean by 'absurd', let us turn to the plant, and enquire how the plant could be absurd. Suppose you came upon an orchid or a cabbage reading Flaubert's *Salammbô* or Plutarch's *Moralia*, you would be very much surprised. But if you found a man or a woman reading it, you would *not* be surprised.[3]

So, if a man behaves like a cabbage, then that is funny, but if a cabbage behaves like a man, then that is also funny. It is incontestable. Person-become-thing and thing-become-person are both funny and therefore both Bergson and Lewis would appear justified in their theories of laughter.

But, beyond this simple reversal of Bergson, there is a deeper point to Lewis's argument. He continues,

> Now in one sense you ought to be just as much surprised at finding a man occupied in this way as if you had found an orchid or a cabbage, or a tom-cat, to include the animal world. There is the same physical anomaly. It is just as absurd externally, that is what I mean. – The deepest root of the Comic is to be sought in this anomaly.[4]

This thought adds an interesting twist to the matter. It is not so much a person behaving like a thing or *vice versa* that is the root of the comic, but rather – surprise, surprise – *a person acting like a person*. That is, there is something essentially ridiculous about a human being behaving like a human being; there is something laughable about me behaving like a little professor of philosophy and you behaving like earnest readers of a book on humour. It is finally absurd, is it not? We might just as well be cabbages.

HOW HUMOUR BEGINS IN PHILOSOPHY

We have now arrived at a fresh formulation of the problem: what is essentially laughable is a person acting like a person. Lewis goes on to give a further vivid example drawn from the London Underground,

> The other day in the underground, as the train was moving out of the station, I and those around me saw a fat but active man run along, and deftly project himself between the sliding doors, which he pushed to behind him. Then he

stood leaning against them, as the carriage was full. There was nothing especially funny about his face or general appearance. Yet his running, neat and deliberate, but clumsy embarkation, *combined with the coolness of his eye*, had a ludicrous effect, to which several of us responded. His *eye* I decided was the key to the absurdity of the effect. It was its detachment that was responsible for this.[5]

In this case, what is ludicrous is simply a person, a fat but fit person, acting just like a person, and executing a difficult manoeuvre with some aplomb. This is funny because of a certain detachment, a disinterested coolness that the man has with respect to both the action he carries out and the fit but fat body that carries out the action. That is to say, everything becomes laughably absurd when I begin to detach myself from my body, when I imagine myself, my ego, my soul, or whatever, in distinction from its corporeal housing. Thinking back to the last chapter, humour takes root in the unbridgeable gap between the physical and the metaphysical, between body and soul, between 'being' and 'having'.

This is how humour begins in philosophy, whether it is Descartes's thought experiment in the *Meditations*, the Cartesian meditations of Husserl, or Thomas Nagel pondering what it is like to be a bat. Reflect for a moment on what Descartes asks of us in his thought experiment in the Second Meditation,

. . . If I look out of the window and see men crossing the square, as I just happen to have done, I normally say that I see the men themselves, just as I say that I see the wax. Yet do I see any more than hats and coats which could conceal *automatons*? I *judge* that they are men. And so something which I thought I was seeing with my eyes is in fact grasped solely by the faculty of judgement which is in my mind.[6]

For Descartes, the judgement that what I am now perceiving are in fact thinking beings like myself, and not automatons, is not something inferred from the evidence of the senses, but rather something that has to be deduced rationally. This is why the philosophical quest for certainty cannot be reduced to a naïve empiricism. For Descartes, philosophy requires a certain detachment of the rational soul from the sensible body, a separation of the metaphysical from the physical. But this philosophical operation is achieved by a momentary transformation of a person into a thing – an automaton – where the living becomes encrusted with the mechanical. In short, it is a comic effect.

In this way, we come back to another of Bergson's central ideas when he writes that what takes place in the comic is 'the body taking precedence over the soul' ('le corps prenant le pas sur l'âme'). He writes,

> Why do we laugh at an orator who sneezes at the most moving part of his discourse? Where lies the comic element in this sentence, taken from a funeral speech and quoted by a German philosopher, 'He was virtuous and plump'. It lies in the fact that our attention is suddenly recalled from the soul to the body.[7]

Or again,

> Napoleon, who was a psychologist when he wished to be so, had noticed that the transition from tragedy to comedy is effected simply by sitting down.[8]

Philosophy begins with the adoption of a contemplative attitude that permits a certain detachment of the soul from the body. In Descartes, there is a separation of the dubitable world of fleeting appearances from an indubitable point of thought that is both the engine of sceptical doubt and the point at which doubt comes to an end. What cannot be doubted is the fact that there is a thinking thing that doubts. Now, it is in this contemplative detachment of the soul from the body that humour takes root as the body taking precedence over the soul. It is only when the soul is detached from the body that the body can take precedence over the soul. What is funny, finally, is the fact of having a body. But to find this funny is to adopt a philosophical perspective, it is to view the world and myself disinterestedly. Jokes are the expression of an *abstract* relation to the world. In hearing a joke, like Wyndham Lewis's man on the London Underground, I suddenly and coolly detach myself from my immediate experience and it is from this contemplative standpoint that the bathetic rationality of humour performs its magic. Descartes famously and perhaps rightly said that one could only do metaphysics for a few hours a year. The great virtue of humour is that it is philosophizing in action, a bright silver thread in the great duvet of existence. And one can easily engage in it for an hour or two every day.

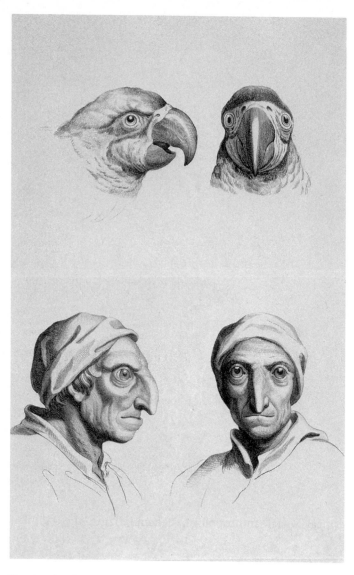

Two heads of parrots and two heads of men in relation to the parrot
Source: Cnac-Mnam/Dist RMN. Charles Le Brun

Foreigners are Funny – the Ethicity and
Ethnicity of Humour

Five

Which one do you think is humorous?
a If we laugh at a third person
b If you laugh at yourself
c If you can get someone else to laugh at themselves.

Max Frisch

Jokes are like small anthropological essays. If one of the tasks
of the anthropologist is to revise and relativize the categories
of Western culture by bumping them up against cultures
hitherto adjudged exotic, then we might say with Henk
Driessen that,

> Anthropology shares with humour the basic strategy of
> defamiliarization: common sense is disrupted, the
> unexpected is evoked, familiar subjects are situated in
> unfamiliar, even shocking contexts in order to make the
> audience or readership conscious of their own cultural
> assumptions.[1]

The lesson that Driessen draws from this is that anthropologists
are akin to comedians, tricksters, clowns or jesters. The lesson
that we can draw from Driessen is that humour is a form of
critical social anthropology, defamiliarizing the familiar,
demythologizing the exotic and inverting the world of common sense. Humour views the world awry, bringing us back
to the everyday by estranging us from it. This is what I
meant above when I claimed that humour provides an oblique

phenomenology of ordinary life. It is a practice that gives us an alien perspective on our practices. It lets us view the world as if we had just landed from another planet. The comedian is the anthropologist of our humdrum everyday lives.

Any study of humour, again like anthropology, requires fieldwork and detailed contextualization. Finally, it is only as good as its examples. And what makes humour both so fascinating and tricky to write about is the way in which the examples continually exceed the theoretical analysis one is able to give of them – they say more in saying less. For Driessen, the lesson to be drawn from anthropology is the humility of a certain cultural relativism, as a strategy aimed at combating the intolerance and racism of Western ethnocentrism. Now, is the same true of humour? Your sense of humour may not be the same as mine – let us hope it is not for both of our sakes – but does the study of humour lead us to embrace cultural relativism?

THE UNIVERSAL AND THE PARTICULAR

With this question, arguably the most intractable dilemma of humour can be broached: the universal *versus* the particular. Most studies of humour, jokes and the comic begin by claiming that humour is universal. Apparently there have never been cultures without laughter, although the varieties and intensities of humour vary dramatically. Mary Douglas writes,

> We know that some tribes are said to be dour and unlaughing. Others laugh easily. Pygmies lie on the ground and kick their legs in the air, panting and shaking in paroxysms of laughter.[2]

However, to say that humour is universal is, of course, to say almost nothing, or very little. All cultures laugh, just as all cultures have a language and most of them seem to have some sort of religious practice usually involving a belief in a hidden metaphysical reality and an afterlife. So what? The fact that all cultures laugh might be a formal universal truth, of the same order as admitting that all human beings eat, sleep, breathe and defecate, but it tells us nothing at the level of a concrete context, and that is where matters begin to get difficult and interesting.

Humour is local and a sense of humour is usually highly context-specific. Anyone who has tried to render what they believe to be a hugely funny joke into a foreign language only to be met by polite incomprehension will have realized that humour is terribly difficult to translate, perhaps impossible. Although various forms of non-verbal humour can travel across linguistic frontiers, witness the great success enjoyed by the *Commedia dell'arte* throughout Europe in the sixteenth and seventeenth centuries and the enduring popularity of various forms of mime and silent comedy, such as Chaplin, Monsieur Hulot and Mr Bean, verbal humour is notoriously recalcitrant to translation. The speed and brevity of wit can become tiresome and prolix in another tongue, and a joke explained is a joke killed. In 1921, Paul Valéry noted, 'Humour is untranslatable. If this was not the case, then the French would not use the word'.[3] But if Valéry is right and the French use humour because it is untranslatable, then might it not be the very untranslatability of humour that somehow compels us? Might not its attraction reside in the fact that it cannot be explained to others, and that humorous *savoir faire* always contains a certain *je ne sais quoi*?

Humour is a form of cultural insider-knowledge, and might, indeed, be said to function like a linguistic defence mechanism. Its ostensive untranslatability endows native speakers with a palpable sense of their cultural distinctiveness or even superiority. In this sense, having a common sense of humour is like sharing a secret code. Indeed, is this not the experience of meeting a compatriot in an otherwise foreign environment, on holiday or at a conference, where the rapidity of one's intimacy is in proportion to both a common sense of humour and a common sense of humour's exclusivity? We wear our cultural distinctiveness like an insulation layer against the surrounding alien environment. It warms us when all else is cold and unfamiliar.

ETHOS AND ETHNOS

If, as I have claimed, humour can be said to return us to physicality and animality, then it also returns us to *locality*, to a specific and circumscribed *ethos*. It takes us back to the place we are from, whether that is the concreteness of a neighbourhood or the abstraction of a nation state. The word *ethos* must here be understood in its ancient Greek sense, as both custom and place, but also as disposition and character. A sense of humour is often what connects us most strongly to a specific place and leads us to predicate characteristics of that place, assigning certain dispositions and customs to its inhabitants. The sweet melancholy of exile is often rooted in a nostalgia for a lost sense of humour.

There is a further link to be made here between *ethos* and *ethnos*, in the sense of a people, tribe, social group or, in the modern world, nation. In relation to humour, this is often vaguely expressed in two ways: first that 'foreigners' do not have a sense of humour; and, second, that they are funny. Such are the powerful basic ingredients of ethnic humour. Recall that George Orwell famously said that the British Empire was based on two fundamental beliefs: 'nothing ever changes', and 'foreigners are funny'.[4] In ethnic humour, the *ethos* of a place is expressed by laughing at people who are not like us, and usually believed to be either excessively stupid or peculiarly canny. In England, the Irish are traditionally described as stupid and the Scots as canny; in Canada, the Newfies and the Nova Scotians assume these roles; in Finland, the Karelians are deemed stupid and the Laihians clever; in India, the Sikhs and the Gujaratis occupy these places. Either way, the belief is that 'they' are inferior to 'us' or at least somehow disadvantaged *because* 'they' are not like 'us'. Such is the menacing flipside of a belief in the untranslatability and exclusivity of humour.[5]

The facts of ethnic humour are all too well known: the French laugh at the Belgiums, the Belgiums laugh at the Dutch, and the Dutch laugh right back. The Danes laugh at the Swedes, the Swedes laugh at the Finns, and the Finns laugh right back. The Scots laugh at the English, and the English laugh at the Irish, and the Irish laugh right back. The Germans laugh at the Ostfrieslanders and everyone else laughs rather nervously at the Germans. In relation to humour, the Germans are obviously a special case and much could be said about anti-German jokes, whose history stretches back at least 200 years; a case that was obviously not helped over-much by the events of the last century. German humour is no laughing matter. Ted Cohen relates a splendidly objectionable joke,

The thing about German food is that no matter how much you eat, an hour later you are hungry for power.[6]

This qualifies as what Cohen calls a 'meta-joke', where the condition for the joke is the fact that you already know the joke about Chinese food invariably leaving one hungry soon after eating. Therefore, this is not just a joke, but a joke about a joke, a sheer play upon form.

It is indeed interesting to note no lesser a personage than George Eliot writing in 1856 in a fascinating essay on the great German wit, Heinrich Heine,

> . . . German humour generally shows no sense of measure, no instinctive tact; it is either floundering and clumsy as the antics of a leviathan, or laborious and interminable as a Lapland day, in which one loses all hope that the stars and quiet will ever come.

Warming to her theme, she continues,

> A German comedy is like a German sentence: you see no reason in its structure why it should ever come to an end, and you accept the conclusion as an arrangement of Providence rather than that of the author.[7]

We should note that Heine got his own back in typical style by describing the English language as the 'hiss of egoism' ('Zischlaute des Egoismus'). Now, such humour is undoubtedly funny. But it is neither innocent, nor to be strongly recommended. The curious feature of the German case is that the alleged absence of a sense of humour has been thoroughly internalized by German culture and one often hears one's German friends bemoaning their lack of a sense of humour.

In my view, the intimate connection between the ethnicity and 'ethicity' of humour must be recognized and not simply sidestepped. Ethnic humour is very much the Hobbesian laughter of superiority or sudden glory at our eminence and the other's stupidity. It is a curious fact that much humour, particularly when one thinks of Europe, is powerfully connected to perceived, but curiously outdated, national styles and national differences. There is something deeply anachronistic about much humour, and it refers nostalgically to a past whose place in the present is almost mythical, certainly fantastical. For good or ill, old Europe still has a robust fantasy life.

THERE WAS A FRENCHMAN, AN ENGLISHMAN AND AN IRISHMAN . . .

Although I have spent many happy hours thumbing its pages, it is always an open question how much etymological authority one should invest in the Oxford English Dictionary. If one consults the entry on 'humour', the OED states that the first recorded usage of the word to indicate something amusing or jocular occurs in 1682. This is obviously not to say that there was no humour prior to that date, but rather that the association of the word 'humour' with the comic and the jocular is an innovation that belongs to a specific time and place: the English language in the late seventeenth century. Prior to that date, humour signified a mental disposition or temperament, as in Ben Jonson's 'Every man in his humour', from 1598. The earlier meaning derived from the ancient Greek medical doctrine of the four humours or fluids that made up and regulated the body: blood, phlegm, bile and black bile (melancolia). It is this link between humour and melancholy that Breton suggests in his notion of humour noir.

Thus, the association of humour with the comic and jocular is specifically modern, and arises in the period of the rise of the modern nation state, in particular the astonishing rise of Britain as a trading, colonizing and warring nation after the establishment of constitutional monarchy in the Glorious Revolution of 1688. This dating will be confirmed in the next chapter when we turn to Shaftesbury's hugely influential treatise on humour from 1709. The modernity of humour is something also apparent in French accounts of the origin of the concept. Although the English word is originally a French borrowing, from the Anglo-Norman humour and the Old French humor, it is curious to note that French dictionaries claim that the modern sense of humour is an English borrowing. The Dictionnaire de l'Académie Française is quite adamant on this point. 'Humour' is a

> Word borrowed from English. A form of irony, at once pleasant and serious, sentimental and satirical, that appears to belong particularly to the English spirit (l'esprit anglais).[8]

With the dissenting voice of Voltaire, who thought that the English had stolen the notion of humour from the comedies of Corneille, French authors in the eighteenth century and as late as Victor Hugo in 1862 refer to 'that English thing they call humour'.[9]

One finds the same view in Diderot's and D'Alembert's Encyclopédie, in a fascinating short article that may have been written by Diderot himself, although the attribution is not certain. 'Diderot' writes,

> HUMOUR: The English use this word to designate an original, uncommon and singular pleasantry. Amongst the authors of that nation, no one possesses humour, or this original pleasantry, to a higher degree than Swift. By the force which he is able to give to his pleasantries, Swift brings about effects amongst his compatriots that one would never expect from the most serious and well-argued works, ridiculum acri, etc. Thus it is, in advising the English to eat little Irish children with their cauliflowers, Swift was able to hold back the English government which was

otherwise ready to remove the last means of sustenance and commerce from the Irish people. This pamphlet has the title, 'A Modest Proposal'.[10]

We should note the exemplary place of Swift in this French history as the 'plus haut point' of English humour. This is something continued in Breton, who begins his anthology of *humour noir* with Swift's 'Modest proposal'. Breton claims Swift as 'the true initiator' of *humour noir*, and as the inventor of 'ferocious and funereal pleasantry' ('la plaisanterie féroce et funèbre').[11] Of course, the question of ethnicity returns once again here, for it is curious, indeed paradoxical, to define humour as something essential to 'l'esprit anglais', and then to give Swift as the highest example of English humour; the Dean was not exactly English. As Beckett replied when he was asked by an American journalist whether he was English: 'au contraire'. The same reply might also apply to Swift, Sterne, Wilde, Joyce and many other Irish contraries to Englishness. But if Irishness is the contrary of Englishness, then it is important to point that it is an internal contradiction. Humour is a battlefield in the relation between what Richard Kearney rightly calls those national Siamese twins, England and Ireland, locked together in a suffocatingly close, often deathly embrace.[12]

HAVING THE COURAGE OF OUR PAROCHIALISM

So, humour is what returns us to our locale, to a specific *ethos* which is often identified with a particular people possessing a shared set of customs and characteristics. A sense of humour is often what is felt to be best shared with people who are from the same place as us, and it is that aspect of social life which is perhaps the most difficult to explain to people from somewhere else. That is to say, humour puts one back in place in a way that is powerfully particular and recalcitrantly relative.

This point is important because we should not, in my view, shy away from the relativistic nature of humour. When it comes to what makes us laugh, 'we must', as Frank Cioffi writes, 'have the courage of our parochialism'.[13] As I have claimed, humour puts us back in place, whether the latter is our neighbourhood, region or nation. Now it *can* do this triumphantly, and this is the basic feature of ethnic humour. However, it *need* not put us back in place in this manner. It might equally put one back in one's place with the anxiety, difficulty and, indeed, shame of where one is from, a little like trying to explain the impotent rage of English football hooligans to foreign friends. Perhaps one laughs at jokes one would rather *not* laugh at. Humour can provide information about oneself that one would rather *not* have.

This phenomenon is probably most sharply revealed in the gap between what one found funny in the past and what one now finds funny. Episodes of Monty Python that had me innocently rolling on the floor in pre-pubescent mirth in the early 1970s, and which we – like so many others – laboriously tried to rehearse word-for-word during lunch breaks at school, now seem both curiously outdated, not that funny, and crammed full of rather worrying colonial and sexist assumptions. Equally, as an eager cosmopolitan, I would rather not be reminded of national differences and national styles, yet our sense of humour can often unconsciously pull us up short in front of ourselves, showing how prejudices that one would rather not hold can continue to have a grip on one's sense of who one is.

In this sense, one might say that the very relativity of humour can function as an (un)timely reminder of who one is, and the nature of what Heidegger would call one's *Geworfenheit*, or thrownness. If humour returns us to our locale, then my point is that it can do this in an extremely uncomfortable way, precisely as thrown into something I did not and would not choose. If humour tells you something about who you are, then it might be a reminder that you are perhaps not the person you would like to be. As such, the very relativity of humour might be said to contain an indirect appeal that this place stands in need of change, that history is, indeed, in Joyce's words, a nightmare from which we are all trying to awake.

COMIC REPRESSION

A similar point can also be made in Freudian terms. In *The Interpretation of Dreams*, Freud makes a very perceptive remark about the relation between the comic and repression,

> Evidence, finally, of the increase in activity which becomes necessary when these primary modes of functioning are inhibited is to be found in the fact that we produce a *comic* effect, that is, a surplus of energy which has to be discharged in *laughter, if we allow these modes of thinking to force their way through into consciousness.*[14]

The claim here is that I produce a surplus of energy in laughter to cope with my inhibition when repressed unconscious material threatens to force its way through into consciousness. For example, my tight-lipped refusal to laugh at an anti-Semitic joke might well be a symptom of my repressed anti-Semitism. As Freud claims, jokes have a relation to the unconscious; they articulate and reveal a certain economy of psychical expenditure. In this sense, ethnic jokes can be interpreted as symptoms of societal repression, and they can function as a return of the repressed. As such, jokes can be read in terms of what or simply who a particular society is subordinating, scapegoating or denigrating. Grasping the nature of societal repression can itself be liberating, but only negatively. As Trevor Griffiths writes, 'A joke that feeds on ignorance starves its audience'.[15]

Two heads of boars and two heads of men in relation to the boar
Source: Cnac-Mnam/Dist RMN. Charles Le Brun

The Joke's on All of Us – Humour as *Sensus Communis*

Six

Tout n'est pas poisson, mais il y a des poissons partout.
(All is not fish, but there are fish all over)

Leibniz, **Letter to Arnauld**, September 1687

Despite the obdurate relativity of humour, let me pose the seemingly odd question: do jokes raise validity claims? That is, are there good reasons for gags, reasons which I would expect to be binding on others? Is there such a thing as comic rationality? The question sounds peculiar as jokes would appear to presuppose none of the conditions for validity formulated by a philosopher like Jürgen Habermas: grammatical well-formedness, truth, rightness, adequacy of standards of value and sincerity.[1] Jokes can be insincere, have highly inadequate standards of value, be empirically wrong, manifestly untrue, and grammatically ill-formed: 'What do Attila the Hun and Winnie the Pooh have in common? They have the same middle name'. Jokes are notoriously recalcitrant to the standards of rationally motivated agreement that Habermas would want to claim for speech acts. For whatever reason, I can always refuse *a priori* to find something funny.

However, the thesis that I would like to pursue is that humour is a form of *sensus communis*, common sense. That is, jokes are the expression of sociality and possess an implicit reasonableness. I will give the grounds for this claim presently, but the essential point here is that humour is shared. Every comedian knows that a joke that does not get a laugh is not a joke – end of story. Of course, if the gag does not get a laugh, then the comic can compensate by adding the rejoinder: 'well, please yourselves', or 'why don't you all join hands and try and make contact with the living', or 'this audience doesn't need a comic, it needs an embalmer'. But that simply confirms negatively the point that humour is a shared or intersubjective practice that requires the assent of others. Of course, one can always opt out of this *sensus communis* for whatever reason. One can, like Queen Victoria, refuse to be amused. But the surprising thing about jokes is that they always presume an intersubjective appeal, they have *social reach*. In Alfred Schutz's terms, jokes, like fantasies and dreams, are acts of abstraction or distancing from ordinary life that reveal the shared structures of a common life-world.[2]

SHAFTESBURY'S REASONABLE RAILLERY

Sensus communis is a Roman concept for which, strangely, there is no natural equivalent in ancient Greek. It would appear that the somewhat artificial Greek term koinonoēmosunē was the coinage of Marcus Aurelius. *Sensus communis* is employed by authors like Horace and Juvenal and is more felicitously rendered as 'sociableness' than 'common sense', which is a term whose too frequent (ab)use invites misunderstanding. For someone like Cicero, *sensus communis* is linked to the notion of *urbanitas* or urbane wit. The term is retrieved in the seventeenth century by Giambattista Vico, but the linking of *sensus communis* to humour is the invention of Anthony, Earl of Shaftesbury, himself completely immersed in Roman culture.[3] His 1709 treatise, *Sensus communis. An Essay on the Freedom of Wit and Humour*, appears just twenty-seven years after the first occurrence of the word 'humour' to denote something jocular.

In an extended epistle to an unnamed friend, Shaftesbury seeks to defend 'true raillery' against the 'defensive raillery' of previous ages. Such raillery can be justified as it makes conversations agreeable but also, more importantly, because it encourages the use of reason. In response to the accusation that humour is the irrational befuddlement of reason, Shaftesbury writes,

> To this I answer, that according to the notion I have of reason, neither the written treatises of the learned, nor the set discourses of the eloquent, are able of themselves to teach the use of it. 'Tis the habit alone of reasoning which can make a reasoner. And men can never be better invited to the habit than when they find pleasure in it. A freedom of raillery, a liberty in decent language to question everything, and an allowance of unravelling or refuting any argument, without offence to the arguer, are the only terms which can render such speculative conversations in any way agreeable.[4]

Thus, raillery and ridicule can be defended insofar as they enable instruction in reason by making its use pleasurable. One is more likely to use reason if its use gives pleasure. Therefore, liberty is precisely a freedom in wit and humour. The measure of liberty to which reason appeals, for Shaftesbury, is *sensus communis*, sociableness. He writes, ' 'Tis the height of sociableness to be friendly and communicative'.[5]

Shaftesbury's implied antagonist is Hobbes, and the treatise contains a most succinct refutation of Hobbes's conception of the state of nature. In a very patrician putdown, Shaftesbury writes, ' 'Tis not fit we should know that by nature we are all wolves'.[6] To Hobbes's suspicion of laughter as 'that passion that hath no name', we can oppose Shaftesbury's notion of humour as the very height of reasonableness, an opposition that is obviously linked to their contrasting political philosophies. Shaftesbury goes so far as to find Hobbes's suspicion of all forms of popular government a distrust of liberty itself. In response to Hobbes's advice to the sovereign that he should extirpate the teaching of Greek and Roman literature, he quips, 'Is not this in truth somewhat Gothic?'[7]

If liberty loves humour, then slavery finds expression in buffoonery. Shaftesbury writes, 'The greater the weight is, the bitterer will be the satire. The higher the slavery, the more exquisite the buffoonery'.[8] Buffonic comedy is a function of, and a reaction to, repression. This explains why, on Shaftesbury's reading, the permitted inversions of the dominant theological and political order in Carnival produce such seemingly disorderly and transgressive humour. But rather than placing in question the dominant order, such acts of comic subversion simply reinstate it by offering transitory comic relief. After Carnival comes Lent, and one cannot exist without the other.

Such an argument against the alleged subversive potential of carnivalesque, buffonic comedy might also be extended to explain the quite vicious comedy of the court, exemplified in the figure of the fool, as he who alone can speak the truth to power. With regard to the historical provenance of the concept of humour, it is significant that the tradition of court jesters does not survive the seventeenth century in England, the last recorded fool being Henry Killigrew appointed to William III in 1694.[9]

More tentatively, a similar point could be made about the often violent humour that existed under totalitarian regimes, a fact which is not incidental, I believe, to the circumstances of composition and indirect intention of Bakhtin's *Rabelais and his World*. Although the latter's ostensive subject matter is the late medieval period in France, the book was written in 1941, just a few years after the height of the Stalinist purges, of which Bakhtin was a long-suffering victim. Bakhtin's defence of what he calls 'grotesque realism', his praise of 'comic heteroglossia', of unofficial culture, of the unruliness of the body and the identification of the latter with the 'collective ancestral ground of the people', is clearly an implied critique of the official culture and hierarchy of Stalinism and its aesthetics of socialist realism.[10]

DISENCHANTMENT OF FOLLY OR DEMOCRATIZATION OF WIT?

We here approach an interesting scansion in the history of the comic, between a religious or courtly tradition of buffoonery and tomfoolery, a tradition that is sustained by the satirical ribaldry that appears (or at least appears to us) to undermine it, and a more secular, democratic use of wit and humour as that which can encourage the use of reason and guide the sociability of *sensus communis*. The way in which the history of the comic is often presented is in terms of a decline in toleration for the ludic, subversive folly of the Christian Middle Ages. One finds, for example, Peter Berger writing, 'Modernity did away with much of the enchantment that medieval man still lived with. The counter-world of folly began to recede . . .'.[11] In this sense, modern European history can be presented as a dour, Protestant taming of the transgressive comedy of a Catholic world. The transition from a medieval-Renaissance world-view to that of modernity is defined in terms of the gradual disappearance of the ludic, playful element in culture.

The problem I have with this historical thesis is that it sounds rather like good, old-fashioned European cultural pessimism *à la* Oswald Spengler dressed up in a jester's cap and bells. We disenchanted moderns are sorely tempted by what appears as comic transgression in the pre-modern period and then sink into a wistful nostalgia for a lost world of Christian folly. But perhaps it is a world well lost. Whatever the truth of the matter, humour is a distinctively modern notion and is linked to the rise of the democratic public sphere in places like Britain in the eighteenth century. However great its powers of disenchantment, one can also approach modernity in terms of a democratization of wit.

But I do not wish to exculpate Shaftesbury. It must not be forgotten that the appeal to *sensus communis* entails certain restrictions on the free use of wit and humour. It has to accord with taste, 'There is a great difference between seeking how to raise a laugh from everything and what justly may be laughed at'.[12] Also, Shaftesbury's conception of the freedom of wit is not particularly democratic, but is rather clubbish and gentlemanly. He writes,

> For you are to remember my friend, that I am writing to you in defence only of the liberty of *the club*, and of that sort of freedom which is taken amongst gentlemen . . .[13]

Finally, and most egregiously, Shaftesbury's defence of humour is served with a large helping of British chauvinism. After noting that 'the greatest of buffoons are the Italians' because ''tis the only manner in which the poor cramped wretches can discharge a free thought', he goes on to praise the British government for its use of common sense to guide politics,

> As for us Britons, thank heaven, we have a better sense of government delivered to us from our ancestors. We have the notion of a public, and a constitution; how a legislative and an executive is modelled (. . .) Our increasing knowledge

On Humour

> shows us everyday, more and more, what common sense is
> in politics; and this must of necessity lead us to understand
> a like sense in morals, which is the foundation.[14]

One wonders what Swift might have made of such wisdom.

INTERSUBJECTIVE ASSENT

The precise extent of the influence of Shaftesbury's theory of wit, humour and *sensus communis* on the aesthetic theory of Kant is an intriguing matter of intellectual history.[15] In the German-speaking milieu, Shaftesbury was avidly read by Lessing and Moses Mendelssohn and it is rather tempting to imagine that in Kant's development of the notion of *sensus communis* in *The Critique of Judgement* one hears at least an echo of Shaftesbury's theory of humour. Sadly, despite Kant's fascinating discussion of laughter, he confines humour to the domain of the agreeable rather than the beautiful, whose analysis is the proper business of aesthetic judgement.[16]

Yet, Kant's basic insight, stripped of all the fascinatingly baroque complexity of *The Critique of Judgement*, is that there is something about the form of aesthetic judgement that requires intersubjective assent or agreement. For Kant, if something merely pleases, then I must not call it beautiful; it is simply charming or agreeable and 'no one cares about that'.[17] However, when I say that this thing is beautiful, then I require and indeed *demand* the agreement of others. Kant tells a powerful story which gives us the analytic conditions for such a propensity to judgement: universality, disinterestedness and what he calls 'purposiveness without purpose'. But the basic point here is that when I express my judgement of taste about an artwork, film or novel, then I require the agreement of others, I crave assent. In my view, this is best revealed in those

The Joke's on All of Us

moments when one leaves a cinema with a friend. One moves silently in the throng with the subtle anxiety of trying to guess what your friend thought of the film: 'so, what did you think?', 'wasn't it brilliant?', or 'wasn't that the biggest turkey the world has ever seen?'. I think matters are analogous with humour. If you do not laugh at my joke, then something has gone wrong either with my joke or with my telling of it. Either way, it is a mistake.

JOKES AS EVERYDAY ANAMNESIS

If that is so, that is, if humour is a form of *sensus communis* that requires intersubjective assent of some sort, then how might we characterize and assess the validity claim of a joke? Now, I do not want to tell a Habermasian or even Kantian story at this point because that would take us in the direction of a universalism that would lose sight of the phenomenon under consideration. I would rather make a more Wittgensteinian point and speak about jokes as clarificatory remarks, that make situations perspicuous, that provide us with some sort of synopsis or overview of a particular state of affairs.[18] In this sense, jokes are further descriptions of phenomena that show them in a new light. They are acts of 'everyday anamnesis', that remind us what we already know in a new way. Humour lights up what Schutz calls the 'stock of knowledge' that we all share.

As such, if we understand jokes as clarificatory remarks, then they are not simply occasions for solipsistic rumination, rather they bring us back to a social world that is common and shared. This is what Cioffi means when he speaks of 'an experiential sense of *thereness* for everyone'.[19] Jokes have a sense of *thereness*; they illuminate a social world that is held in common with others. If we are to clarify this *thereness*, then it must be in terms of the 'we' of a specific community, with a common language and shared cultural assumptions and life-world practices. In this sense, jokes are reminders of who 'we' are, who 'we' have been, and of who 'we' might come to be. This is what was meant in the last chapter by having the courage of our parochialism. Jokes can do this in at least two ways, by either reinforcing our sense of cultural distinctiveness and superiority, as in much ethnic humour, or by placing those shared practices in question, showing them in a new light, by taking the comedy of recognition and turning the whole thing on its head. For a comedian like Eddy Izzard, a simple trip to the launderette turns into a surreal phantasmagoria, with clothes taking on personalities and Eddy's socks arriving half an hour late, complaining about being stuck in traffic and demanding to be let into the washing machine.

ANAESTHESIA OF THE HEART

The genius of jokes is that they light up the common features of our world, not by offering theoretical considerations, or by writing the two admirably fat volumes of Habermas's *The Theory of Communicative Action*, but in a more practical way. They are forms of practical abstraction, socially embedded philosophizing. Jokes light up specific practices, such as going to the launderette, in a practically abstract manner. Laughter gives us a distance on everyday life, and there is a certain coldness at its core. I think this is what Bergson means – and it is a deep remark – when he speaks of the comic as demanding 'something like a momentary anaesthesia of the heart'.[20] Jokes are forms of abstraction that place in abeyance our usual modes of reaction, whether veridical or moral: if someone falls on a banana skin, then we do not rush to help, we sit back and laugh; if a horse talks, then we do not express disbelief, but delight. That is, humour lets us take up a disinterested, theoretical attitude towards the world, but it does this in an eminently practical and interesting way.

The comedian sees the world under what some philosophers call an *epochē*, a certain bracketing or suspension of belief. Of course, this can be the *epochē* of delusion, as in the comedy of Don Quixote, where the simple denizens of the Spanish countryside become noble knights and damsels in distress. The comedian behaves like a visitor from another planet, vainly trying to disappear into practices that we take for granted, and failing calamitously in the process – one thinks of Monsieur Hulot. But we watch the comic from a this-worldly perspective, like Sancho Panza, enjoying the delusory *epochē* from a certain distance, where we can suspend reality, and yet still engage in reality testing. The comedian is psychotic, whereas his audience are simply healthy neurotics.

But if there is a coldness at the core of the comic, then this can also be disturbing, as in the case of *humour noir*. Consider the Coen Brothers' 1996 film, *Fargo*, where multiple murder is treated with a troubling numbness that is accentuated through the complete inarticulacy of any of the film's protagonists to provide a motivation or justification for their actions. There is a complete disjunction of action and affect here, a sheer anaesthetization of death. Yet, such lack of sentimentality does not leave us cold, but paradoxically has the effect of emphasizing the sheer horror of the events being depicted.

THE PHENOMENOLOGY OF PHENOMENOLOGY

If jokes are best thought of as clarificatory remarks whose validity is resolved in an appeal to *sensus communis*, then what is required is not some causal or quasi-scientific theory that attempts to explain jokes in genetic, evolutionary or physiological terms. In my view, this is where Freud goes wrong in the 1905 *Jokebook*, where he seeks to explain jokes causally in terms of his hydraulic model of the psyche. Cioffi puts the point colourfully by asking us to enter into a thought experiment,

> Imagine a world in which, like ours, people laughed at jokes, but unlike ours did not know what they were laughing at until they discovered the unconscious energic processes hypothesised by Freud – only after peering through the psychoanalytoscope were they able to pronounce – 'Just as we thought: a classic case of condensation with slight modification'. You would then have a picture of the world Freud intermittently beguiled himself (and us) into believing he was living in and which prompts Wittgenstein's attempts to wake us by reminding us of its unreality – 'a powerful mythology'. We can't escape the conclusion that Freud's theoretical pronouncements are only redescriptions of the phenomena they purport to explain. What makes them 'good representations of the facts', as Wittgenstein puts it, are Freud's perceptiveness and expressive powers.[21]

Happily, as I shall argue presently, Freud's later remarks on humour are a distinct improvement on his early position and testify to his great perceptiveness and expressive powers.

In my view, what is required in the face of humour are further descriptions on the role of jokes as further descriptions, remarks of the kind that Wittgenstein made about Freud on jokes, 'All we can say is that if it is presented to you, you say "Yes, that's what happened"'.[22] What we require is a phenomenology of the phenomenology of the world that jokes provide. Such a phenomenology of phenomenology might have the virtue of allowing us to separate the occasions on which we require causal scientific explanations from those occasions when we do not, that is, when the situation demands a more humane clarification. Such is the ambition of this book.

Yet, that still begs the following question: if humour is defined by the limits of the 'we' to whom the joke is concerned, if a sense of humour is relative to a shared but specific life-world, then is all humour reactionary and conservative? Most of it is, and maybe humour will always be dominated by laughing at others, at other *ethnoi* with other *ethoi*. As I said above, such humour has to be recognized, even if it is not to be recommended. Nonetheless, I would like to propose a counter-thesis, what I will describe as my sense of humour. I want to defend a two-fold claim: first, that the tiny explosions of humour that we call jokes return us to a common, familiar domain of shared life-world practices, the background meanings implicit in a culture. This is what is meant by humour as a form of *sensus communis*, where jokes can be seen to raise intersubjective validity claims of the kind described above. However, second, I want to claim that humour also indicates, or maybe just adumbrates, how those practices might be transformed or perfected, how things might be otherwise. That is, humour might be said to project another possible *sensus communis*, namely a *dissensus communis* distinct from the dominant common sense. In laughing at a joke I am also consenting to a certain ideal image of the world. In this sense, as I argued in my Introduction, laughter has a certain messianic power. Let me illustrate this obliquely with a joke,

> In the old days, somewhere in Eastern Europe, a traveller arrived in a *shtetl* in the middle of winter. There, outside the synagogue, an old man sat on a bench, shivering in the cold.
>
>   'What are you doing here?' asked the traveller.
>
>   'I'm waiting for the coming of the Messiah.'

'That is indeed a very important job', said the traveller. 'I suppose that the community pays you a good salary?'

'No, not at all', said the old man. 'They don't pay me anything. They just let me sit on this bench. Once in a while someone comes out and gives me a little food.'

'That must be very hard for you', said the traveller. 'But even if they don't pay you anything, surely they must honour you for undertaking this important task?'

'No, not at all', said the old man. 'They all think that I'm crazy.'

'I don't understand this', said the traveller. 'They don't pay you. They don't respect you. You sit here in the cold, shivering, hungry. What kind of job is this?'

The old man replied: 'It's *steady work*.'[23]

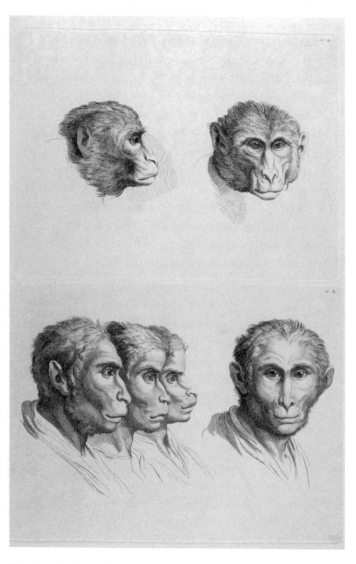

Two heads of monkeys and four heads of men in relation to the monkey
Source: Cnac-Mnam/Dist RMN. Charles Le Brun

Why the Super-Ego is Your Amigo – My Sense of Humour and Freud's

Seven

> Perhaps I know best why man alone laughs: he alone suffers so
> deeply that he had to invent laughter. The unhappiest and most
> melancholy animal is, as is fitting, the most cheerful.
>
> Nietzsche

In his seventy-fifth year, looking back nearly a third of a century to the publication of *The Interpretation of Dreams* in 1900, Freud wrote, 'Insight such as this falls to one's lot but once in a lifetime'.[1] Unfortunately for his readers, Freud could not leave that insight alone throughout his lifetime. He kept fretfully going back to his *magnum opus*, fiddling with it anxiously, revising, expanding and adding sections, multiplying footnotes. This is what gives the book its rather flabby feel, which makes it, in my experience, a difficult though rewarding text to teach. One of the curious things about the 1905 *Jokes and Their Relation to the Unconscious*, is that Freud never really went back to it, or indeed expressed that much interest in its main topic in the years after its publication. Oddly, given that topic, the *Jokebook* is arguably the most systematic of Freud's works, with a neat and clear tripartite division into 'analytic', 'synthetic' and 'theoretic' parts. Contrary to popular prejudice, it is also full of wonderful, if occasionally objectionable, jokes: 'what is it that men do standing up, women do sitting down and dogs do on three legs?' (I presume you know the answer.) So, it was after a gap of some twenty-two years that Freud sat down for five days in August 1927 to pen a paper on humour,

93 **On** Humour

simply called 'Der Humor'.[2] Now, as even professional anti-Freudians acknowledge, quite a bit happened to Freud's views during the intervening twenty-odd years. Thus, much of the curiosity of the 1927 paper stems from how the phenomenon of the comic looks from the perspective of Freud's later theory of mind, namely what is called the second topography of ego, super-ego and id. So, how does it look?

FINDING ONESELF RIDICULOUS

With the telegraphic conciseness of his late style, Freud shows how the phenomenon of humour is the contribution made to the comic by the super-ego. Recall that the thesis of the *Jokebook* is that jokes are the contribution of the unconscious to the comic. What this means is that in humour, the super-ego observes the ego from an inflated position, which makes the ego itself look tiny and trivial. The core insight of the paper is that in humour I find myself ridiculous and I acknowledge this in laughter or simply in a smile. Humour is essentially self-mocking ridicule. The importance of this claim for my purposes is that Freud's sense of humour provides me with the normative criterion for my own sense of humour: namely, the distinction between laughing at oneself and laughing at others. As we saw in the discussion of ethnic humour, laughing at others has to be recognized, but is not to be recommended.

As always when he is at his best, Freud is detained and perplexed by an empirical item, in this case a joke, a case of what André Breton would call at the end of the 1930s, directly inspired by the 1927 paper, l'*humour noir*. In a real sense, all Freudian humour – indeed, all humour – is replete with the unhappy black bile, the *melan-cholia*. Freud speaks of a criminal who, on the morning of his execution, is being led out to the gallows to be hanged, and who remarks, looking up at the sky, 'Na, die Woche fängt gut an', 'Well, the week's beginning nicely'.[3] Freud asks himself: why is this funny? How is this funny? In the language of the second topography, the humour here is generated by the super-ego observing the ego, which produces un humour noir that is not depressing but rather liberating and elevating. Freud's precise words are befreiend, erhebend. He concludes the little essay on humour with the following words, 'Look! Here is the world, which seems so dangerous! It is nothing but a game for children, just worth making a jest about'.[4]

So, humour consists in laughing at oneself, in finding oneself ridiculous, and such humour is not depressing, but on the contrary gives us a sense of emancipation, consolation and childlike elevation. The childlike aspects of humour are important and serve to bring out an interesting contrast between Freud's sense of humour and his early theory of jokes. He writes,

> Humour possesses a dignity which is wholly lacking, for instance, in jokes, for jokes either serve simply to obtain a yield of pleasure or place the yield of pleasure that has been obtained in the service of aggression.[5]

Freud is here unwittingly inheriting the Hobbesian tradition of the superiority theory of laughter discussed above. For Freud, Oedipalist that he was, the core of this superiority theory of laughter consists in the fact that in laughing at another's misfortune, I treat them as a child and myself as an adult.

Now, in adopting a humorous attitude towards myself it is precisely the other way around: I treat myself as a child from an adult perspective; I look at my childlike, diminutive ego from the standpoint of the big, grown-up super-ego. And it is for this reason that Freud says that humour possesses a dignity or worth, *eine Würde*, that is lacking in jokes. That is, in jokes I laugh at others, find them ridiculous and myself superior. From a Freudian point of view, such laughter has to be analysed because it reveals all sorts of unresolved psychological conflict which ultimately – surprise, surprise – has a sexual aetiology. Thus, my excessively hearty laughter in the bar with the boys at a series of aggressively homophobic gags would be read by Freud symptomatically as the expression of a repressed desire to sleep with some or maybe all of those boys. Such laughter has to be analysed because it tells us much about the nature of unconscious aggression, but Freud is clear that it is not to be recommended. Therefore, humour for Freud – and in my view he is right in this – is ethically superior to the laughter of superiority expressed in jokes: laughter at oneself is better than laughter at others. This normative priority of humour over jokes can also be linked, as we will see presently, to the priority of smiling over laughter.

SUBJECT AS ABJECT OBJECT

So, how does humour fit into the landscape of the second topography and how, as I think it does, might humour be said to change that landscape? Let us conduct a brief survey of the terrain. In my view, the key insight that inaugurates the second topography is the splitting of the ego initially outlined in Freud's 1914 essay, 'On narcissism: an introduction'. But, for reasons that will soon become obvious, let me explain this briefly with reference to Freud's discussion of melancholia from the following year. About five pages into 'Mourning and melancholia', Freud speculates on the origin of conscience. He writes of the depressive that,

> We see how in him one part of the ego sets itself over against the other, judges it critically, and, as it were, takes it as its object. Our suspicion that the critical agency which is here split off from the ego might also show its independence in other circumstances will be confirmed by every further observation. We shall really find grounds for distinguishing this agency from the rest of the ego. What we are here becoming acquainted with is the agency commonly called 'conscience'; we shall count it, along with the censorship of consciousness and reality-testing, among the major institutions of the ego and we shall come upon evidence that it can become diseased on its own account.[6]

Freud here resolves a perplexity sketched earlier in the essay: namely, that if mourning is the response to the death of the beloved – what he somewhat cruelly calls 'object-loss' – then to what is melancholia a response, given that no one has died, that is, seemingly there was no object to lose? This perplexity is resolved by the fact that in melancholy the 'ego itself becomes an object'. What this means is that there is a splitting in the ego between the ego and a critical agency, the Über-Ich, the 'over-I' or 'super-ego' that stands over against the Ich, sadistically denigrating it. This is what Freud calls 'conscience', das Gewissen, the etymological semantics of which resonate in the Middle English notion of 'Inwit', recalled by Joyce, alluding to Langland, as the 'Agenbite of Inwit', the again-biting or guilty call of conscience. Thus the ego does not only become an object, it becomes what we might call an abject object, and it is with this insight that the third agency of the psyche, the super-ego, is born.

The subject becomes an abject object, and when the melancholic talks about himself it is as though he were talking about some loathsome thing. This is why melancholics talk so obsessively about themselves; in a sense, they are talking about somebody else. If they experience themselves as worthless, then they do this in the noisiest and most wearisome way. One is reminded of Woody Allen's endless monologues, where he complains about himself in the most voluble manner, a technique of self-objectification and splitting of the ego brought to dramatic perfection in *Play it Again Sam*, where the super-ego who lacerates and consoles the abject Allen ego is literally objectified in the person of Humphrey Bogart.

MELANCHOLY PHILOSOPHERS

Now, whatever the reality of the accusations that the melancholic levels against himself – and an essential feature of Woody Allen's comedy is their obvious unreality – Freud concludes that there is no point contradicting him. We must accept his description as the right one for his psychological situation. Furthermore, Freud goes on in an interesting move, the melancholic might after all be *justified* in these accusations; namely, that he has achieved a higher degree of self-knowledge than the rest of us. Freud writes,

> When in his heightened self-criticism he describes himself as petty, egoistic, dishonest, lacking in independence, one whose sole aim has been to hide the weaknesses of his own nature, it may be, so far as we know, that he has come pretty near to understanding himself; we only wonder why a man has to be ill before he can be accessible to a truth of this kind.[7]

In short, the melancholic has deeper self-knowledge than other people, which raises the fascinating question as to why one should have to be sick to possess such insight. As Aristotle realized some millennia ago, the melancholic is a philosopher and the philosopher is a melancholic. One begins to compile a list of philosopher-melancholics with the names of Montaigne and Pascal scribbled at the top, but which would also include many others, perhaps even some of this book's readers. Freud illustrates the pathology of the philosopher-melancholic with the example of Hamlet, whose abjection is mirrored in the ghostly object of his father. We might also think of Dostoevsky's underground man as the paradigm case of melancholic self-insight. Freud wrote his fascinating study of Dostoevsky in the same year as his paper on humour, in 1927, where the super-ego and the parricidal identification with the father figures prominently.[8]

As Wittgenstein often reminds us, philosophy is indeed a kind of sickness. But perhaps the sickest thought is the belief that there is a cure for this malady through some spurious return to health, whether by simply leaving one's college and taking a walk into town, or by renouncing philosophy altogether and wandering back into the thickets of common sense. The melancholic philosophical ego is constituted in relation to what Freud calls 'an unknown loss', a narcissistic wound that imperceptibly rubs under one's clothes, irritating and agitating the ego. Because of this wound, the philosopher-melancholic – and one thinks of the late Nietzsche of *Ecce Homo* with chapters entitled 'Why I am so clever', 'Why I am a destiny' – experiences himself in a radical non-self-coincidence, as an abject object. This is why a sense of humour is essential in philosophy.

MANIC INTOXICATION

Melancholy shares many traits with normal mourning, apart from one, namely the loss of self-regard and the accompanying feeling of worthlessness. This is diagnosed by Freud as a regression from what he calls 'object libido' to 'narcissistic libido', that is to say, from a relation to a beloved to a relation to self. It is this regression that splits the ego and produces conscience or the super-ego. The originality of the phenomenon of melancholy is that once investment or 'cathexis' in the object has been withdrawn, then the poles of subject and object are interior to the ego, or rather they are poles of a splitting in the ego where the latter itself becomes the object that is hated and treated sadistically. At this point, my self-insight and self-criticism can turn into the much nastier phenomena of self-hatred, and self-punishment.

In the 1915 essay, the escape from the self-hatred of melancholia lies in its counter-concept, *mania*. Freud writes, 'The most remarkable characteristic of melancholia . . . is its tendency to change around into mania'.[9] Here we have a classic example of what Freud describes in his essay on the drives – which is the first in the series of papers of which 'Mourning and melancholia' is the last – as an instinctual vicissitude, where something reverses into its opposite, the way love can flip over into hate, sadism into masochism, voyeurism into exhibitionism.[10] As such, mania is the same as melancholia insofar as they are opposed manifestations of the same complex, the only difference being that in melancholy the ego succumbs to the complex, whereas in mania it pushes it aside. Freud insists that manic states such as joy, exaltation and triumph depend on the same psychical energy as melancholia. Freud's 'economic' speculation is that the discharge of energy which is suddenly available and free in mania and experienced as exaltation and joy, is the same energy that was bound and inhibited in melancholia. The point here is that melancholia and mania are two ends of the same piece of string, and the relation between them is powerfully ambivalent. Melancholia can alternate with mania, sometimes within a single evening. Interestingly, this is Freud's explanation of alcoholic intoxication, where the manic elation of drunkenness is followed by the melancholy self-laceration of the hangover – a claim that I am sure that some of you have tested empirically.

HUMOUR AS ANTI-DEPRESSANT

After having now surveyed the second topography a little, let me go back to the paper on humour in order to see how that landscape might be reshaped a little. In 1927, looking over his shoulder to the arguments of the 1915 essay, Freud writes of 'The alternation (*die Abwechslung*) between melancholia and mania, between a cruel suppression of the ego by the super-ego and a liberation of the ego after that pressure . . .'. And it is here that the originality of the paper on humour can be seen, for Freud's remarks on humour constitute an unexpected development of the internal logic of narcissism which finds a positive place for the super-ego. The narcissistic splitting of the ego does not only produce the alternating pathologies of melancholia and mania, with their endless to and fro, but also produces humour – dark, sardonic, wicked humour: 'well, the week's beginning nicely'. In addition to the self-laceration of depression and the self-forgetfulness of elation – the morning after and the night before, as it were – there is a third way, namely humour. Humour has the same formal structure as depression, but it is an anti-depressant that works by the ego finding itself ridiculous. This can be illustrated with a favourite joke of Groucho Marx, which he relates in his autobiography,

> I'm sure most of you have heard the story of the man who
> tells an analyst he has lost the will to live. The doctor
> advises the melancholy figure to go to the circus that night

and spend the evening laughing at Grock, the world's funniest clown. 'After you have seen Grock, I am sure you will be much happier.' The patient rises to his feet and looks sadly at the doctor. As he starts to leave the doctor says, 'By the way, what is your name?' The man turns and regards the analyst with sorrowful eyes.

'I am Grock.'[11]

The subject looks at itself like an abject object and instead of weeping bitter tears, it laughs at itself and finds consolation therein. Humour is an anti-depressant that does not work by deadening the ego in some sort of Prozac-induced daze, but is rather a relation of self-knowledge. Humour is often dark, but always lucid. It is a profoundly *cognitive* relation to oneself and the world.

I would argue that humour recalls us to the modesty and limitedness of the human condition, a limitedness that calls not for tragic-heroic affirmation but comic *acknowledgement*, not Promethean authenticity but a laughable inauthenticity.[12] Maybe, we have to conclude with Jack Nicholson in the 1997 movie of the same name, this is as good as it gets. And that realization is not an occasion for moroseness but mirth. The anti-depressant of humour works by finding an alternative, positive function for the super-ego, and it is this thought that I would like to explore.

SUPER-EGO I AND II

Some versions of psychoanalysis, and most versions of the ethics of psychoanalysis, have a problem with the super-ego. This is not surprising as it is the super-ego that generates the hostility towards the ego that crystallizes into the symptom. It is the position of the lacerating super-ego that the analyst has to occupy if the analysis is going to proceed with any success. Thus, the patient has to substitute the destructive relation towards the super-ego with a positive transference towards the analyst in order to break down the symptom. In the penultimate paragraph of the paper on humour, Freud acknowledges that 'In other connections we knew the super-ego as a severe master'. However – and this is what is so interesting about the 1927 paper – what is evinced or glimpsed in humour is a non-hostile super-ego, a super-ego that has undergone what we might call 'maturation', a maturity that comes from learning to laugh at oneself, from finding oneself ridiculous. We might say that in humour the childlike super-ego that experiences parental prohibition and Oedipal guilt is replaced with a more grown up super-ego, let us call it 'super-ego II'. Now, this super-ego is your amigo. Freud writes in the final paragraph of the 1927 paper,

> If it is really the super-ego which, in humour, speaks such kindly words of comfort to the intimidated ego, this will teach us that we still have a great deal to learn about the nature of the super-ego.[13]

True enough, Freud and his commentators have said many inconsistent things about the super-ego. My point, however, is simple: in humour, we see the profile of 'super-ego II', a super-ego which does not lacerate the ego, but speaks to it words of consolation. This is a positive super-ego that liberates and elevates by allowing the ego to find itself ridiculous. If 'super-ego I' is the prohibiting parent, scolding the child, then 'super-ego II' is the comforting parent. Or better still, 'super-ego II' is the child that has become the parent: wiser and wittier, if slightly wizened.

IDEAL SICKNESS

Yet, if that is so, then is 'super-ego II' not playing the role normally given to what Freud calls 'the ego ideal'? No, it is not. And I think we need to distinguish the super-ego from the ego ideal, a distinction that was not always respected by Freud. After initially distinguishing the ego ideal from the critical agency of conscience in the 1914 essay on narcissism, he came to identify the ego ideal with what was baptized the super-ego from 1923 onwards in *The Ego and the Id*. So, how should the distinction be made? I think that Annie Reich gets it about right in saying that 'The ego ideal represents what one wishes to be, the super-ego what one ought to be'.[14] That is, the ego ideal is the phantasy of a wish that I would like to see fulfilled. By contrast, the super-ego is a more normative agency which tells me what I should be, which is something which might most often simply conflict with the ego ideal. For example, I might still wish to play soccer for Liverpool FC, but I know that I really should carry out my duties as a philosophy professor. The ego ideal is the heir to what Freud calls 'primary narcissism', that is, the infantile illusion of omnipotence and the blissful feelings bound up with it. On a psychoanalytic view, the function of perversion is to bridge the gap between the ego and the ego ideal and, as it were, to restore the God-like majesty of the baby. The ego ideal is centred on the infantile belief that I am superman, I am a destiny, or am just somehow rather special. Such is what Janine Chasseguet-Smirgel calls 'the malady of the ideal', a sickness with which we are all more or less afflicted.

By contrast, the super-ego is not the heir to primary narcissism, but to the Oedipus complex, and the parental or symbolic prohibition to which the resolution of the complex gives rise. It can be a very severe master. My claim is that, on the one hand, humour makes the super-ego a less severe master, permitting a maturation of the super-ego function that can have extremely salutary effects. On the other hand, I think that 'super-ego II' is what takes the place of the ego ideal, and all the fantasies of primary narcissism: perversion, ecstasy, superman affirmation, fusion with God or your essential self, and a legion of other chimeras. Finally, perhaps it is the super-ego that saves the human being from tragic hybris, from the Promethean fantasy of believing oneself omnipotent, and it does this through humour. For, I am Grock, and you are too. Chasseguet-Smirgel writes,

> To accept the super-ego is to place oneself within a tradition, to become a link in a chain, to resign oneself also to being a human being. To be a superman is to refuse all that en bloc, that is, to refuse the human condition.[15]

LAUGHTER I AND II

Our self-understanding can be transformed, then, if we learn to laugh. But there is laughter *and* laughter. On the one hand, there is the laughter of what Nietzsche calls 'eternal return', the golden laughter of tragic affirmation, that so influenced Georges Bataille and his epigones.[16] This is the heroic laughter that rails in the face of the firing squad – 'Go ahead, shoot me, I don't care'. This is the laughter that I always suspect of emanating from the mountain tops, from the cool summits of lofty isolation. This is precisely a *manic* laughter in Freud's sense: solitary, juvenile, perverse, verging on sobbing. This is the ego bloated and triumphant in empty solitude and infantile dreams of omnipotence. As Beckett quips in his *Proust*, ' "Live dangerously", that victorious hiccup in vacuo, as the national anthem of the true ego exiled in habit'.[17] 'Live dangerously',

what does that mean? At best, you might end up like Austin
– Danger is my middle name – Powers.

On the other hand, there is a weaker Freudian laughter, that
is also, as my epigraph shows, present in Nietzsche. Such
laughter insists that life is not something to be affirmed
ecstatically, but acknowledged comically. This is the sardonic
and more sarcastic comedy of someone like Sterne, Swift or
Beckett, which arises out of a palpable sense of inability,
impotence and inauthenticity. For me at least – although
there is no accounting for taste – it is this second laughter
that is more joyful (not to mention being a lot funnier), and
also more tragic. As Beckett's Malone remarks, paralysed in
his death-bed, 'If I had the use of my body I would throw
it out of the window. But perhaps it is the knowledge of my
impotence that emboldens me to that thought.' This is quintessentially oxymoronic Beckett: the condition of possibility
for the hypothesis 'if . . . then . . .' is an impossibility. Beckett's
sentences proceed by falling apart in what he calls his 'syntax
of weakness'. As I suggested above, this is a comic syntax:
Groucho with his hand on Chico's pulse, 'either this man is
dead or my watch has stopped'.

Let me give you two examples of a Freudian sense of
humour with a pair of anecdotes: one concerns the French
Jewish philosopher, Emmanuel Levinas, the other concerns the
Hungarian philosopher and aesthetician, György Lukács. As
many of you will know, Lukács was not a great admirer of the
work of Franz Kafka, whom he declared to be an 'idealist' and
a bad example of decadent aesthetic modernism. Now, Lukács
was Minister of Culture in the Hungarian government in 1956,
at the moment when the Soviet tanks rolled into Budapest.
Lukács was arrested in the middle of the night and thrown into
a military lorry along with other government officials. The

lorry then disappeared off into the obscurity of the countryside for an appointment with an unknown but probably unsavoury fate. So the story goes, Lukács turned to one of the other ministers and said in German, 'Tja, Kafka war doch ein Realist' ('Kafka was a realist after all'). The essential feature of this joke is that in this situation, which is extremely bleak, Lukács ironizes himself. The humour consists in the fact that Lukács finds himself ridiculous because reality has conspired to bring about a situation which directly contradicts his aesthetic judgement, something which he admits willingly. It is similar in the second story, even if the situation is somewhat more quotidian. A French colleague of mine, Alain David, was taking tea with Levinas at the latter's apartment on the Rue Michel-Ange in Paris. After having finished their first cup of tea, Alain David asked, 'Monsieur, est-ce que vous en voulez une autre?', and Levinas answered, 'Non merci, je suis mono-thé-iste'. Once again, the essential feature of the joke is that Levinas was indeed a rather observant monotheist. Thus, the humour is here directed by Levinas against himself, he finds himself ridiculous. Both these anecdotes remind me of the great Tommy Cooper gag, 'So I got home, and the phone was ringing. I picked it up, and said "Who's speaking please?" And a voice said "You are"'.

SMILING – THE MIND'S MIME

Such anecdotes, it is true, make us laugh out loud. But when they are recalled or ruminated upon they also cause us to smile ruefully, even wistfully. It is this smile of knowing self-mockery and self-ridicule that interests me and that I would like to discuss in closing. George Meredith writes of, 'that slim feasting smile, shaped like a long-bow, was once a big round satyr's laugh'. Yet, it is this finely tempered smile that is, for him, the 'sunlight of the mind, mental richness rather than noisy enormity'.[18] In an aphorism entitled 'Laughter and smiling', Nietzsche makes an analogous point,

> The more joyful and certain the mind becomes, the more we learn to forget loud laughter and put in its place a continual spirited smiling, a sign of its astonishment at the countless hidden comforts of a good existence.[19]

In many languages, smiling is a diminutive of laughter. In Latin, one distinguishes *ridere* from *subridere*, laughter from sub- or under-laughter. The same is true in French and Italian: *rire* and *sourire*, *ridere* and *sorridere*. In German, one has the distinction between *das Lachen* and *das Lächeln*, or 'little laughter'. This is also present in Swedish in the distinction between *skratta* and *småskratta*, and elsewhere. In English, being the bastard bunch that we are, 'laughter' comes from the shared old Germanic root, whilst 'smile' comes from the Danish *smile* or *smila*, which also means 'small laugh'.

Smiling differs from laughter because it lacks the latter's explosiveness. It is silent and subdued. The smile speaks, but not out loud. Its eloquence is reticent. The noisy physicality of laughter is substituted by a more gentle play of the facial features. The simple creasing of the lines around the eyes and mouth in smiling at once deepens, softens and opens the face. Smiling is comic relief that throws the face into relief, signifying a break in our usual flow of inhibitions. A smile, it is true, can mark the beginning or end of a laugh, but it can also take its place. Physical existence is framed by the smile of a new born baby and that which follows our death-throes.

Although he does not actually mention smiling, Freud notes that 'It is true that humorous pleasure never reaches the intensity of the pleasure in the comic or in jokes, that it never finds vent in hearty laughter'.[20] So, the yield of pleasure in humour is quite small. It is certainly not the buffonic back-slapping Rabelaisian guffaw of the carnivalesque, but rather the modesty of the chuckle or the humble smirk. Yet, for me, it is the smile that is powerfully emblematic of the human, the quiet acknowledgement of one's limitedness.

In a wonderful essay, Plessner calls smiling the mind's mime, *die Mimik des Geistes*.[21] What he means by this is that smiling, like thinking, assumes a certain distance from one's immediate surroundings and even from one's body, as we saw above. There is restraint and discretion in the smile. It is an expression that takes up a certain distance from expression – a diminutive expression. As such, I would wager, a smile is the mark of the eccentricity of the human situation: between beasts and angels, between being and having, between the physical and the metaphysical. We are thoroughly material beings that are unable to *be* that materiality. Such is the curse of reflection, but such also is the source of our dignity. Humour is the daily bread of that dignity.

THE *RISUS PURUS*

I shall leave the final words to Beckett, whose early hero Belacqua counted all the smiles in Dante's *Commedia*. Now, there are many significant smiles in Beckett.[22] For example, in *Watt*, our hero is described in terms which echo my discussion of peditological humour,

> Watt's smile was further peculiar in this, that it seldom
> came singly, but was followed after a short time by another,
> less pronounced it is true. In this it resembled the fart. And
> it even sometimes happened that a third, very weak and
> fleeting, was found necessary, before the face could be at

rest again. But this was rare. And it will be a long time now
before Watt smiles again, unless something very
unexpected turns up, to upset him.[23]

Again, in *Molloy* where Moran is hallucinating Youdi's words to
Gaber,

Gaber, Gaber, he said, life is a thing of beauty, Gaber, and a
joy for ever. He brought his face nearer mine. A joy for ever,
he said, a thing of beauty, Moran, and a joy for ever. He
smiled. I closed my eyes. Smiles are all very nice in their
own way, very heartening, but at a reasonable distance.
I said, Do you think he meant human life?[24]

One also thinks of the broad smile, 'toothless for preference',
that cuts across the listener's face at the end of the 1976
dramatic piece 'That Time'.[25] But perhaps the most intriguing
smile does not belong to one of Beckett's 'gallery of mori-
bunds', but to Beckett himself. It is taken from a non-fictional
text that was written for Radio Éireann (although there is no
record of it ever having been broadcast) in June 1946. Beckett
reflects upon his experiences working in an Irish Red Cross
hospital in St-Lô, Normandy, after the devastation of the D-Day
landings. After an intense Allied bombardment, St-Lô changed
hands between the Germans and the Americans for six weeks
and was referred to by the locals as 'the capital of the ruins'.
Towards the end of the account, Beckett writes,

What was important was not our having penicillin when they
had none, nor the unregarding munificence of the French
Ministry of Reconstruction (as it was then called), but the
occasional glimpse obtained, by us in them and, who knows,
by them in us (for they are an imaginative people), of that
smile at the human conditions as little to be extinguished by

> bombs as to be broadened by the elixirs of Burroughs and
> Welcome, – the smile deriding, among other things, the
> having and the not having, the giving and the taking,
> sickness and health.[26]

For me, it is this smile – deriding the having and the not having, the pleasure and the pain, the sublimity and suffering of the human situation – that is the essence of humour. This is the *risus purus*, the highest laugh, the laugh that laughs at the laugh, that laughs at that which is unhappy, the mirthless laugh of the epigraph to this book. Yet, this smile does not bring unhappiness, but rather elevation and liberation, the lucidity of consolation. This is why, melancholy animals that we are, human beings are also the most cheerful. We smile and find ourselves ridiculous. Our wretchedness is our greatness.

ONE INTRODUCTION

1 *The Philosophy of Laughter and Humour*, ed. John Morreall (State University of New York Press, Albany, 1987).

2 Henri Bergson, *Laughter* (The Johns Hopkins University Press, Baltimore, 1980), p.65.

3 Ludwig Wittgenstein, *Culture and Value*, ed. G. H. Von Wright (Blackwell, Oxford, 1980), p.83.

4 Mary Douglas, 'Do dogs laugh?' and 'Jokes' from *Implicit Meanings. Essays in Anthropology* (Routledge, London, 1975).

5 Kundera, *The Book of Laughter and Forgetting* (Penguin, London, 1983), pp.232–3.

6 Immanuel Kant, *The Critique of Judgement*, trans. J. C. Meredith (Oxford University Press, Oxford, 1952), pp.196–203.

7 Philip Larkin, *High Windows* (Faber, London, 1974), p.11.

8 Laurence Sterne, *The Life and Opinions of Tristram Shandy, Gentleman*, eds. M. and J. New (Penguin, London, 1997), p.58.

9 Helmuth Plessner, 'Das Lächeln', in *Mit anderen Augen. Aspekte einer philosophischen Anthropologie* (Reclam, Stuttgart, 1982), p.185.

10 Jacques Le Goff, 'Laughter in the Middle Ages', in Jan Bremmer and Herman Roodenburg (eds), *A Cultural History of Humour* (Polity, Cambridge, 1997), p.45.

11 Trevor Griffiths, *Comedians* (Faber, London, 1976), p.20.

12 André Breton, *Anthologie de l'humour noir* (Jean-Jacques Pauvert, Paris, 1966).

13 Douglas, *Implicit Meanings*, op.cit. p.96.

14 I have benefited from correspondence with Samantha Arnfeld on this point. I also learnt a great deal from conversations at Witten-Herdecke University in Germany with Dirk Baecker and Frank Dievernich.

15 Jonathan Swift, *Selected Poems*, ed. C. H. Sisson (Carcanet, Manchester, 1977), pp.85–6.

16 Cited in *The Restoration and the Eighteenth Century*, ed. M. Price (Oxford University Press, Oxford, 1973), p.236.

17 M.A. Screech, *Laughter at the Foot of the Cross* (Penguin, London, 1997).

18 'Concerning the unpredictable', in *Forewords and Afterwords* (Faber, London, 1973), p.472. My thanks to Peter Howarth for alerting me to this passage.

19 Peter L. Berger, *Redeeming Laughter. The Comic Dimension of Human Experience* (De Gruyter, Berlin and New York, 1997), p.210.

20 Theodor Adorno, *Minima Moralia* (Verso, London, 1974), p.247.

21 From various Marx Brothers' scripts, Peter Chelsom's wonderful 1994 film *Funny Bones*, and Samuel Beckett's *Endgame* (Faber, London, 1958).

22 *The Life and Opinions of Tristram Shandy, Gentleman*, op.cit. p.58.

TWO IS HUMOUR HUMAN?

1 Chapter X, p.29.

2 *Molloy*, from *The Beckett Trilogy* (Picador, London, 1979), p.93.

3 See Screech, *Laughter at the Foot of the Cross* (Penguin, London, 1997). Thanks to Peter Howarth for his correspondence on this question.

4 *Implicit Meanings*, op.cit. pp.83–9.

5 See 'Autobiographische Einführung' and 'Der Mensch als Lebewesen' from *Mit anderen Augen. Aspekte einer philosophische Anthropologie* (Reclam, Stuttgart, 1982).

6 I owe this formulation to Sue Wiseman.

7 Christopher Smart, *Selected Poems*, ed. K. Williamson and M. Walsh (Penguin, London, 1990), pp.105–8.

8 Jonathan Swift, *The Complete Poems*, ed. P. Rogers (Yale University Press, New Haven and London, 1983), p.514.

9 Cited in Berger, *Redeeming Laughter*, p.55.

10 Petronius, *Satyricon*, ed. and trans. R. Bracht Branham (Everyman, London, 1996), p.66.

11 Will Self, *Great Apes* (Bloomsbury, London, 1997), p.15.

12 In *Tough, Tough Toys for Tough, Tough Boys* (Bloomsbury, London, 1998), pp.23–42.

13 *Culture and Value*, op.cit. p.78.

14 See the first of the television programmes that Deleuze recorded for the

Franco-German channel Arte in the last years of his life: 'A comme animal', in *L'Abécédaire de Gilles Deleuze* (Vidéo Editions Montparnasse, Paris, 1997).

15 Thomas Bernhard, *Stücke 2* (Suhrkamp, Frankfurt a.M., 1988), pp.273–4.

16 Cited in Raymond Geuss's hugely entertaining *Parrots, Poets, Philosophers and Good Advice* (Hearing Eye, London, 1999), p.8.

THREE LAUGHING AT YOUR BODY – POST-COLONIAL THEORY

1 See Johan Huizinga, *Homo Ludens: A Study of the Play-Element in Culture* (Beacon Press, Boston, 1955). And see Jacques Le Goff, 'Laughter in the Middle Ages', in *A Cultural History of Humour*, op.cit. pp.40–53.

2 *Redeeming Laughter*, op.cit. p.46.

3 The film is *Carry on Cleo* from 1962, and recall Caesar's apostrophe, 'Infamy, infamy, they've all got it in for me'. For Williams's final words, see *The Kenneth Williams Diaries*, ed. Russell Davies (HarperCollins, London, 1993), p.801.

4 Mikhail Bakhtin, *Rabelais and His World*, trans. Helene Iswolsky (Indiana University Press, Bloomington, 1984), see Chapter 6.

5 Will Self, *Cock and Bull* (Bloomsbury, London, 1992), p.54.

6 *Gulliver's Travels* (Penguin, London, 1967), p.130.

7 *The Works of Geoffrey Chaucer*, ed. F. N. Robinson (Oxford University Press, Oxford, 1957), p.54.

8 I owe this felicitous expression to Gregg Horowitz, who replied to an earlier version of my ideas on humour at Vanderbilt University in March 1998.

9 Rabelais, *Gargantua*, trans. T. Urquhart and P. Motteux (Bodley Head, London, 1927), Vol.1, p.51.

10 Swift, *The Complete Poems*, op.cit. p.466.

11 Beckett, *Molloy, Malone Dies, The Unnameable* (Picador, London, 1979), p.30.

12 *Molloy, Malone Dies, The Unnameable*, op.cit. p.179.

13 On these points, see Aaron Gurevich, 'Bahktin and his theory of carnival', in *A Cultural History of Humour*, pp.54–60. Also, see Steven Connor's excellent, 'Art, criticism and laughter: Terry Eagleton on aesthetics', unpublished typescript. Connor shows how preoccupied Eagleton's work has been with the question of laughter and decisively

argues that this is based on a curious overestimation of the work of Bakhtin, where, for Eagleton, laughter is always identified with the force of the body. Thus, the Bakhtinian heroization of corporeality and materiality is continued in Eagleton's aesthetic theory.

14 *High Windows*, p.19.
15 Cited in James Knowlson, *Damned to Fame. The Life of Samuel Beckett* (Bloomsbury, London, 1996), p.170.

FOUR THE LAUGHING MACHINE – A NOTE ON BERGSON AND WYNDHAM LEWIS

1 Henri Bergson, *Laughter*, op.cit. p.97.
2 Breton, *Anthologie de l'humour noir*, op.cit. p.14.
3 In Wyndham Lewis, *The Complete Wild Body* (Black Sparrow Press, Santa Barbara, 1982), pp.158–9.
4 Ibid, p.159.
5 Ibid, p.159.
6 Descartes, *Meditationes de prima philosophia* (Vrin, Paris, 1978), pp.31–2.
7 Bergson, *Laughter*, op.cit. p.93.
8 Ibid, p.94.

FIVE FOREIGNERS ARE FUNNY – THE ETHICITY AND ETHNICITY OF HUMOUR

1 'Humour, laughter and the field: reflections from anthropology', *A Cultural History of Humour*, p.227.
2 *Implicit Meanings*, op.cit. p.84.
3 Cited in *Le Grand Robert de la Langue Française*, 10th Edition, Paris, 1985, Vol. 5, p.288. This text by Valéry is also briefly discussed in the Preface to Breton's *Anthologie de l'humour noir*, op.cit. p.11.
4 'Boys' Weeklies' from *Inside the Whale and Other Essays* (Penguin, London, 1957), p.187.
5 On ethnic humour, the definitive study is Christie Davies's *Ethnic Humor Around the World* (Indiana University Press, Bloomington, 1990), which is a rich, compendious and extremely helpful work. Davies provides a thorough taxonomy of ethnic humour, persuasively identifying surprisingly common patterns amongst ethnic jokes from all across the world that can be divided into jokes about the stupid and canny.

Therefore, despite the undoubted relativity of the butt of jokes in different contexts, their form remains remarkably similar. Davies outlines the same argument in 'Stupidity and rationality: jokes from the iron cage', *Humour in Society* (Macmillan, Basingstoke, 1988), pp.1–32, where he views jokes about stupidity not as ethnic jokes viciously directed towards hated others, but as a reaction to the excessive rationalization of society. As such, ethnic jokes can be forms of protest. Personally, I have my doubts.

6 Ted Cohen, *Jokes. Philosophical Thoughts on Joking Matters* (University of Chicago Press, Chicago, 1999), p.21.

7 George Eliot, 'German wit: Heinrich Heine', in *Selected Essays, Poems and Other Writings*, ed. A.S. Byatt and N. Warren (Penguin, Harmondsworth, 1990), p.73.

8 Huitième Edition, Hachette, Paris, 1935, p.29.

9 Bremmer and Roodenburg, *A Cultural History of Humour*, pp.1–2.

10 *Encyclopédie, Nouvelle impression en facsimile de la première edition de 1751–80* (Fromann Verlag, Stuttgart-Bad Cannstatt, 1967), Vol. VIII, p.353.

11 Breton, *Anthologie de l'humour noir*, pp.19–21.

12 See Richard Kearney, *On Stories* (Routledge, London, 2002).

13 Cioffi, *Wittgenstein on Freud and Frazer* (Cambridge University Press, Cambridge, 1998), p.18.

14 Freud, *The Interpretation of Dreams*, trans. J. Strachey (Penguin, London, 1976), p.766.

15 *Comedians*, op.cit. p.23.

SIX THE JOKE'S ON ALL OF US – HUMOUR AS *SENSUS COMMUNIS*

1 Jürgen Habermas, *The Theory of Communicative Action*, Vol. 1 (Polity, Cambridge, 1984), pp.18–23 and 38–42.

2 Alfred Schutz, *The Structures of the Life-World* (Northwestern University Press, Evanston, 1963), pp.21–35.

3 On this history of the idea of *sensus communis*, see Gadamer, *Truth and Method* (Sheed and Ward, London, 1975), pp.19–25.

4 In *Characteristics of Men, Manners, Opinions, Times*, Vol. 1–2 (Bobbs-Merrill, New York, 1964), p.49.

5 Ibid, p.62.

6 Ibid, p.63.

7 Ibid, p.61.

8 Ibid, p.51.

9 On this point, see Derek Brewer, 'Prose jest-books mainly in the sixteenth to eighteenth centuries in England', in Bremmer and Roodenburg, *A Cultural History of Humour*, op.cit. pp.104–6.

10 On this point, see Katerina Clark and Michael Holquist, *Mikhail Bakhtin* (Harvard University Press, Cambridge, Mass., 1984), pp.295–320.

11 Berger, *Redeeming Laughter*, op.cit. p.215.

12 Shaftesbury, op.cit. p.85.

13 Ibid, p.53.

14 Ibid, p.73.

15 On this topic, see Jean-Paul Larthomas, *De Shaftesbury à Kant* (Didier Erudition, Paris, 1985); and Fabienne Brugère, *Le gout. Art, passions et société* (Presses Universitaires de France, Paris, 2000), which has a useful chapter on Shaftesbury (pp.31–61).

16 Kant, *The Critique of Judgement*, trans. J. C. Meredith (Oxford University Press, Oxford, 1952), p.203.

17 Ibid, p.52.

18 I am indebted to Frank Cioffi on this point. See his *Wittgenstein on Freud and Frazer* (Cambridge University Press, Cambridge, 1998).

19 Ibid, pp.6–7.

20 Bergson, *Laughter*, op.cit. p.64.

21 Cioffi, *Wittgenstein on Freud and Frazer*, op.cit. p.277.

22 Cited in Cioffi, op.cit. p.266.

23 Cited in Peter Berger, *Redeeming Laughter*, op.cit. p.xvii.

SEVEN WHY THE SUPER-EGO IS YOUR AMIGO – MY SENSE OF HUMOUR AND FREUD'S

1 'Preface to the third revised English edition', *The Interpretation of Dreams* (Penguin, London, 1976), p.56.

2 In Freud, *Standard Edition* Vol. XXI (Hogarth Press, London, 1961), pp.161–6; all page references are to this edition. The essay is also included in the Penguin Freud Library, Vol. 14, *Art and Literature* (Penguin, London, 1985), pp.426–33. I have been unable to find much secondary literature on this essay. There is a good introduction by Peter Gay to the German edition of *Der Witz und seine Beziehung zum Unbewussten* (Fischer, Frankfurt a.M., 1992), which concludes with a discussion of

the 1927 paper. There is a collection of French papers, *L'Humour dans l'oeuvre de Freud* (Editions Two Cities, Paris, 1989). To be frank, with the exception of Daniel Rosé's 'L'humour selon le triple point de vue', these papers are sadly not much use and rather too fond of jargon and cliquish self-reference. Gilles Deleuze makes good use of Freud's essay in his presentation of Sacher-Masoch's *Venus in Furs*, where he advances the intriguing claim that the masochistic relation to law and prohibition is essentially humorous (see Deleuze and Sacher-Masoch, *Masochism* (Zone Books, New York, 1991), pp.87–8 and 124–6).

3 Ibid, p.161.

4 Ibid, p.166.

5 Ibid, p.163.

6 'Mourning and melancholia' in Penguin Freud Vol. 11, *On Metapsychology* (Penguin, London, 1984), p.256.

7 Ibid, p.255.

8 'Dostoevsky and parricide', in Freud, *On Art and Literature*, op.cit. pp.437–60.

9 'Mourning and melancholia', op.cit. p.262.

10 'Instincts and their vicissitudes', in *On Metapsychology*, op.cit. pp.113–38.

11 Cited in Stefan Kanfer, *Groucho. The Life and Times of Julius Henry Marx* (Penguin, London, 2000), p.432.

12 I borrow the concept of acknowledgement from Stanley Cavell. Although it is all over his work, see his 'Knowing and acknowledging' from *Must We Mean What We Say?* (Cambridge University Press, Cambridge, 1976), pp.238–66. One finds an analogous run of argument, linking remorseful mourning to the comic as part of a critique of heroism, in Rowan Williams, *Lost Icons. Reflections on Cultural Bereavement* (T&T Clark, Edinburgh, 2000), pp.129–38.

13 Op. cit. p.166.

14 Cited in Janine Chasseguet-Smirgel's excellent book, *The Ego Ideal*, trans. P. Barrows (Free Association, London, 1985), p.170. I owe this reference to Joel Whitebook.

15 Ibid, p.187.

16 For an example of an approach to laughter inspired by Bataille, see Mikkel Borch-Jacobsen, 'The laughter of being', in *Bataille: A Critical Reader* (Blackwell, Oxford, 1998), pp.146–66.

17 Beckett, *Proust and Three Dialogues* (Calder, London, 1949), pp.8–9.

18 George Meredith, *An Essay on Comedy* (The Johns Hopkins University Press, Baltimore, 1980), pp.47–8.

19 From *Human all too Human*, cited in Stefan Dietzsch (ed.), *Luzifer lacht. Philosophische Betrachtungen von Nietzsche bis Tabori* (Reclam, Leipzig, 1993), p.25.

20 Freud, 'Humour', op.cit. p.166.

21 'Das Lächeln', in *Mit anderen Augen* (Reclam, Stuttgart, 1982), pp.183–97.

22 I would like to thank Theo Bertram for his invaluable research on smiles in Beckett and for sending me his paper 'Beckett's mere smiles'.

23 *Watt*, op.cit. p.25

24 *Molloy*, op.cit. pp.151–2.

25 In *Samuel Beckett. The Complete Dramatic Works* (Faber, London, 1986), p.395.

26 Beckett, 'The capital of the ruins', in *As the Story was Told: Uncollected and Late Prose* (Calder, London, 1990), pp.17–28.

Bibliography

Adorno, Theodor, *Aesthetic Theory* (Athlone, London, 1997).

Arnfeld, Samantha, 'Organizing humour: the ethics of humour as a management tool', Lecture, Trinity College Cambridge, December 2000.

Bakhtin, Mikhail, *Rabelais and his World*, trans. H. Iswolsky (Indiana University Press, Bloomington, 1984).

Beckett, Samuel, *Watt* (Calder, London, 1970).

—— *Molloy, Malone Dies, The Unnameable* (Picador, London, 1979).

—— *The Complete Dramatic Works* (Faber, London, 1986).

—— *As the Story was Told: Uncollected and Late Prose* (Calder, London, 1990).

Berger, Peter, *Redeeming Laughter. The Comic Dimension of Human Experience* (Walter De Gruyter, Berlin and New York, 1997).

Bergson, Henri, *Le rire* in *Œuvres*, Second Edition (Presses Universitaires de France, Paris, 1963), pp.381–485.

—— *Laughter* (The Johns Hopkins University Press, Baltimore, 1980).

Bernhard, Thomas, 'Immanuel Kant', in *Stücke 2* (Suhrkamp, Frankfurt a.M., 1988).

Bohrer, Karl Heinz, *Plötzlichkeit* (Suhrkamp, Frankfurt a.M., 1981).

Borch-Jacobsen, Mikkel, 'The laughter of being', in *Bataille: A Critical Reader* ed. F. Botting and S. Wilson (Blackwell, Oxford, 1998), pp.146–66.

Bremmer, Jan and Roodenburg, Herman (eds), *A Cultural History of Humour* (Polity, Cambridge, 1997).

Breton, André, *Anthologie de l'humour noir* (Jean-Jacques Pauvert, Paris, 1966).

Brugère, Fabienne, *Le gout. Art, passions et société* (Presses Universitaires de France, Paris, 2000).

Cavell, Stanley, *Must We Mean What We Say?* (Cambridge University Press, Cambridge, 1976).

Chasseguet-Smirgel, Janine, *The Ego Ideal. A Psychoanalytic Essay on the Malady of the Ideal*, trans. P. Barrows (Free Association, London, 1985).

Cioffi, Frank, *Wittgenstein on Freud and Frazer* (Cambridge University Press, Cambridge, 1998).

Clark, Katerina and Holquist, Michael, *Mikhail Bakhtin* (Harvard University Press, Cambridge, Mass., 1984).

Cohen, Ted, *Jokes* (University of Chicago Press, Chicago, 1999).

Connor, Steven, 'Art, criticism and laughter: Terry Eagleton on aesthetics', Lecture at 'Aesthetics, gender, nation', University of Oxford, March 1998.

Davies, Christie, *Ethnic Humour Around the World* (Indiana University Press, Bloomington, 1990).

Davies, Russell (ed.), *The Kenneth Williams Diaries* (HarperCollins, London, 1993), p.801.

Deleuze, Gilles with Parnet, Claire, *L'Abécédaire de Gilles Deleuze* (Vidéo Editions Montparnasse, Paris, 1997).

Deleuze, Gilles and von Sacher-Masoch, Leopold, *Masochism* (Zone Books, New York, 1991).

Descartes, René, *Meditationes de prima philosophia* (Vrin, Paris, 1978).

Dietzsch, Stefan (ed.), *Luzifer lacht. Philosophische Betrachtungen von Nietzsche bis Tabori* (Reclam, Leipzig, 1993).

Dollimore, Jonathan, *Sexual Dissidence* (Oxford University Press, Oxford, 1991).

Douglas, Mary, 'Do dogs laugh?' and 'Jokes', in *Implicit Meanings. Essays in Anthropology* (Routledge, London, 1975).

Edwards, Paul, *Wyndham Lewis, Painter and Writer* (Yale University Press, New Haven, 2000).

Eliot, George, 'German wit: Heinrich Heine', in *Selected Essays, Poems and Other Writings* ed. A. S. Byatt and N. Warren (Penguin, Harmondsworth, 1990).

Freud, Sigmund, *The Interpretation of Dreams* (Penguin, London, 1976).

—— *Jokes and Their Relation to the Unconscious* (Penguin, London, 1976).

—— *On Metapsychology* (Penguin, London, 1984).

—— 'Humour' in *Art and Literature* (Penguin, London, 1985), pp.427–33.

—— *Der Witz und seine Beziehung zum Unbewußten. Der Humor* (Fischer, Frankfurt a.M., 1992).

Gadamer, Hans-Georg, *Truth and Method* (Sheed and Ward, London, 1975).

Geuss, Raymond, *Parrots, Poets, Philosophers and Good Advice* (Hearing Eye, London, 1999).

Habermas, Jürgen, *The Theory of Communicative Action*, Vol. 1, trans. T. McCarthy (Polity, Cambridge, 1984).

Honneth, Axel and Joas, Hans, *Social Action and Human Nature* (Cambridge University Press, Cambridge, 1980).

Kanfer, Stefan, *Groucho. The Life and Times of Julius Henry Marx* (Penguin, London, 2000).

Kant, Immanuel, *The Critique of Judgement*, trans. J. C. Meredith (Oxford University Press, Oxford, 1952).

Koch, Gertrud, 'Das Lautlose Lachen im Käfig des Bildes – Jacques Tatis Konstruktionen des Komischen', in *Die Filme von Jacques Tati* (Raben, München, 1984).

Kołakowski, Leszek, *Metaphysical Horror* (Penguin, London, 2001).

Kundera, Milan, *The Book of Laughter and Forgetting* (Penguin, London, 1983).

Larkin, Philip, *High Windows* (Faber, London, 1974).

Lewis, Wyndham, *The Complete Wild Body* (Black Sparrow Press, Santa Barbara, 1982).

Mascha, Efharis, *Ethnic Humour. A Comparative Analysis of the British/Irish and the Greek/Pontian Case*, MA Dissertation in Sociology, University of Essex, 2000.

Meredith, George, *An Essay on Comedy* (The Johns Hopkins University Press, Baltimore, 1980).

Morreall, John (ed.), *The Philosophy of Laughter and Humor* (SUNY, Albany, 1987).

Palmer, Jerry, *Taking Humour Seriously* (Routledge, London, 1994).

—— 'Permission to joke: some implications of a well-known principle', in *Semiotica* 110–11/2 (1996), pp.23–36.

Paul, Jean, *Vorschule der Ästhetik* (Meiner, Hamburg, 1990).

Pensky, Max, 'Remembering natural history – reflections on method and morality in Adorno', unpublished typescript (1997).

Plessner, Helmuth, 'Das Lächeln', in *Mit anderen Augen. Aspekte einer philosophischen Anthropologie* (Reclam, Stuttgart, 1982).

—— *Lachen und Weinen, Gesammelte Schriften*, Vol. 7 (Suhrkamp, Frankfurt a.M., 1984).

Powell, Chris and Paton, George E. C. (eds), *Humour in Society. Resistance and Control* (Macmillan, Basingstoke, 1988).

Ritter, Joachim, 'Über das Lachen', in *Luzifer Lacht*, op.cit. pp.92–118.

Schutz, Alfred, *The Structures of the Life-World*, trans. R. Zaner and H. Tristram Engelhardt (Northwestern University Press, Evanston, 1973).

Screech, M. A., *Laughter at the Foot of the Cross* (Penguin, London, 1997).

Self, Will, *Cock and Bull* (Bloomsbury, London, 1992).

—— *Great Apes* (Bloomsbury, London, 1992).

—— *Tough, Tough Toys for Tough, Tough Boys* (Bloomsbury, London, 1998).

Shaftesbury, Anthony, Earl of, 'Sensus Communis; an essay on the freedom of wit and humour', in *Characteristics of Men, Manners, Opinions, Times*, Vol. 1–2 (Bobbs-Merrill, New York, 1964).

Shentoub, S. A., *L'Humour dans l'oeuvre de Freud* (Edition Two Cities, Paris, 1989).

Skinner, Quentin, *Reason and Rhetoric in the Philosophy of Hobbes* (Cambridge University Press, Cambridge, 1996).

Smart, Christopher, *Selected Poems* ed. K. Williamson and M. Walsh (Penguin, London, 1990).

Snodgrass, Mary Ellen, *Encyclopaedia of Satirical Literature* (ABC-CLIO, Santa Barbara, 1996).

Sterne, Laurence, *The Life and Opinions of Tristram Shandy, Gentleman* ed. M. and J. New (Penguin, London, 1997).

Swift, Jonathan, *Gulliver's Travels* (Penguin, London, 1967).

—— *Selected Poems* ed. C. H. Sisson (Carcarnet, Manchester, 1977).

Wittgenstein, Ludwig, *Culture and Value* (Blackwell, Oxford, 1980).

Thanks

Many audiences in all sorts of places have suffered me talking about humour over the last few years, and I hereby promise not to do so anymore. Enough is enough. Having had the good fortune to speak publicly about humour, I must confess that a lot of the research for this book was done by my auditors, who gave, sent or emailed many precious references that the reader will find scattered throughout this book. Worse still, many of my third-year undergraduate and graduate students at Essex, Paris and elsewhere have been forced to suffer my awful jokes, and it is a token of their humanity that they fed me better lines than I fed them, which are also scattered here and there.

As for specific thanks, I must repay a number of outstanding debts: to Cecilia Sjöholm, for bearing my jokes with patience and discussing all the arguments in this book with me; to Elliot Jurist for strict Freudian comic therapy particularly at the beginning of this project; to Joel Whitebook, Bernard Flynn, Gregg Horowitz, Judith Walz and Max Pensky for their sharp feedback on a version of Chapter 6, which was presented in December 2000 to the American Philosophical Association in New York; to Tony Bruce at Routledge for his constant support with this book and with the series of which it forms part; to my partner-in-crime, Richard Kearney; to Roger Moss, who will find some of his ideas reflected back to him in Chapter

2; to Frank Cioffi, who will find something familiar in Chapter 6. I would also like to thank people who have given me various texts and references at different times, sometimes without realizing it: David Hannigan, Erica Fudge, Theo Bertram, Shohini Chauduri, Jonathan Dollimore, Moira Gatens, Peter Howarth, Keith Ansell-Pearson, Greg Fried, Efharis Mascha, Laura Salisbury, Chris Ellis, Bob Vallier, Sue Wiseman and Alain David. Thanks finally to Laura Hopkins for providing a conclusion of sorts: 'Pas de lieu Rhône que nous'.

Although it very well might not, indeed should not, and hopefully does not appear so, this book is the flipside of an earlier book of mine, called *Very Little . . . Almost Nothing* (Routledge, 1997). Although the latter is all about death and appears rather sombre, this book might appear less sombre. But appearances can be deceptive.

The publisher would like to thank the Réunion des Musées Nationaux and the Chalcographie du Louvre for permission to reprint the illustrations in this book from: *De la Physionomie Humaine et Animale: Dessin de Charles Le Brun gravés pour la Chalcographie du musée Napoléon en 1806*, Paris: Éditions de la Réunion des Musées Nationaux, 2000.

Index

abjection 96–8, 102
abstraction 87–8
Adorno, Theodor 19, 36
Aesop 29, 31
alienation 43
Allen, Woody 98
anaesthesia 87–8
anamnesis 86–7
Anaxagoras 25
Animal Farm 31
animals 25, 27–31, 34–8, 41–3
anthropology 2, 5, 17, 27–8, 65–6
anti-depressants 101–2
anti-Semitism 75
Aristotle 2, 25, 98–9
assent 85–6
Auden, W. H. 16–17

Bakhtin, Mikhail 44, 51, 82
Batailles, Georges 105
bathos 6–7, 37, 47
Baudelaire, Charles 9
Beckett, Bill 52
Beckett, Samuel 25, 32–3; ethnicity 57, 73; post-colonal theory 47–50, 52; super-ego 105–6, 109–11

being 42–5, 109
Berger, Peter 17, 31–2, 42, 83
Bergson, Henri 2, 4, 25; laughing machine 55–9, 61; *sensus communis* 87
Bernhard, Thomas 36–7
bestiality 29–31
Bible 26–7, 42
Blazing Saddles 48
body 7–9, 41–52, 60
Bogart, Humphrey 98
Breton, André 9–10, 31; ethnicity 71, 73; laughing machine 57; super-ego 94
Britain 68–9, 71–3, 84–5
Brooks, Mel 48
buffoonery 82, 83

Cana, wedding at 26
Carnival 82
cartoons 14, 31, 55–6
cathexis 100
Catholicism 83
Chaplin, Charlie 57–8, 67
Chasseguet-Smirgel, Janine 104–5
Chaucer, Geoffrey 29, 46
chauvinism 84–5
Chelsom, Peter 50

Christianity 9, 16–18, 83–4
Cicero 1, 28, 80
Cioffi, Frank 74, 86, 89
Cleese, John 44
cock and bull stories 7, 21–2, 29
Coen Brothers 88
Cohen, Ted 69
Comedians 9–10
commedia dell'arte 51, 67
conscience 96–7
Cooper, Tommy 107
Corneille, Pierre 72
Critique of Judgement, The 85
culture 28–9, 51, 65–8, 83, 87

D-Day 110
Dadaism 37
D'Alembert, Jean Le Rond 72
Dante 109
David, Iain 107
Deleuze, Gilles 35
depression 50–2, 101–2
Descartes, René 8–9, 21, 42, 60–2
detachment 60–2
deterritorialization 35
Dictionnaire de l'Académie Française 72
Diderot, Denis 72
digressions 20–2
disenchantment 83–5
disgust 31–4
dissensus communis 18–20, 90
Don Quixote 56, 88
Dostoevsky, Fyodor 99
Douglas, Mary 5, 10, 27, 66
Driessen, Henk 65
dualism 42

Ecce Homo 99

eccentricity 27–9, 36, 41, 43
Ego and the Id, The 103
Eliot, George 70
Encyclopédie 72
epochē 88
Erasmus 9, 16
ethics 102
ethnicity 3, 12, 65–76, 94
ethnocentrism 66
ethnos 68–73
ethology 28
ethos 68–73
Europe 15, 67, 70–1
explosions 8–9, 16, 90

Falstaff, Sir John 51
Far Side, The 31
Fargo 88
feminism 11
film 43, 48, 50; sensus communis
    85–6; silent 57, 67
Flaubert, Gustave 58
fools 82
France 67, 69, 72–3, 83
Freud, Sigmund 2–3, 9, 49;
    ethnicity 75; laughing machine
    55; sensus communis 88–9; super-
    ego 93–111
fun 12–14
Funny Bones 50

Galen 25
Germany 69–70, 85
Gnosticism 44
grammar 79
Great Apes 31, 32–3
Griffiths, Trevor 9–10, 76
Gulliver's Travels 15, 30–1, 36,
    45

Habermas, Jürgen 79, 86–7
Ham 27
Hamlet 99
Hardy, Oliver 57
having 42–5, 109
Hazlitt, William 25
Hebrew 41–2
Heidegger, Martin 75
Heine, Heinrich 70
history 2
Hobbes, Thomas 2, 6, 12; ethnicity 70; *sensus communis* 81–2; super-ego 95
homophobia 96
Horace 31–4, 80
Hugo, Victor 72
Huizinga, Johan 41
Hulot, Monsieur 44, 88
humans 27–9
l'*humour noir* 10, 71, 73, 88, 94–5
Hungary 106–7
Husserl, Edmund 60
Hutcheson, Francis 3
hydraulic model 89

Immanuel Kant 37–8
incongruity theory 2, 3
Interpretation of Dreams, The 75, 93
intersubjective assent 85–6
intoxication 101
Ireland 72–3
irony 2, 72
Izzard, Eddie 87

Jesus Christ 25–6
Jokebook 89, 93, 94
jokes 1–7; anamnesis 86–7; dignity 96; ethnicity 69; examples 10–12, 19; good/bad 14–16; humanity 31–2; laughing machine 57; phenomenology 3–6, 66, 89–91; *sensus communis* 79–91; super-ego 93, 95, 101–2, 106; unconscious 93–111
Jokes and Their Relation to the Unconscious 55, 93
Jonson, Ben 71
Joyce, James 73, 75, 97
Jubilate Agno 30
Juvenal 31–4, 80

Kafka, Franz 31, 35, 106–7
Kant, Immanuel 3, 5–6, 36–8, 48, 85–6
Kearney, Richard 73
Keaton, Buster 57
Kierkegaard, Søren 3, 17
Killigrew, Henry 82
Kundera, Milan 5

Langland, William 97
language issues 87, 108
Larkin, Philip 6, 51
Larson, Gary 31
laughter 7–9, 14, 16–18; body 41–52; humanity 25; humans 27–9; language issues 108; machines 55–62; mirthless 49–50, 52; self-understanding 105–7
Laurel, Stan 57
Le Goff, Jacques 9
Leibniz, Gottfried Wilhelm von 37
Lessing, Gotthold Ephraim 85
Levinas, Emmanuel 106, 107

Lewis, Wyndham 58–9, 62
liberation 9–10, 76
Life of Brian, The 26
literary history 2
Lloyd, Harold 57
locality 68
London Underground 59–60, 62
Lorenz, Konrad 27
Lowell, James Russell 3
Lukács, György 106–7

machines 55–62
Man and His Dog, A 27
Man Meets Dog 27
management consultants 12–14
mania 99–101, 105
Mann, Thomas 27
Marcus Aurelius 80
Marx Brothers 19, 57, 101–2, 106
maturation 103, 105
Meditations 60
melancholia 68, 71, 94, 96–101
Mendelssohn, Moses 85
Meredith, George 107–8
messianism 16–18, 26, 90–1
meta-jokes 69–70
Metamorphosis 31
metaphysics 43–5, 50–2, 60, 62, 67, 109
Middle Ages 9, 83
Miller's Tale, The 46
Milton, John 6
miracles 26
mirthless laughter 49–50, 52
Modern Times 57
Molloy 47–9, 110
Montaigne, Michel E. de 99
Monty Python 26, 74

Morreall, J. 2–3
mourning 99–100
Münchhausen, Baron Von 56

Nagel, Thomas 60
narcissism 96, 99–101, 104–5
Nero, Emperor 32
Nicholson, Jack 102
Nietzsche, Friedrich 52, 99, 105–6, 108
Noah 26–7
Nun's Priest's Tale, The 29

object-loss 97
Oedipus 95, 103–4
On the Parts of Animals 25
Oratore, De 1
Orwell, George 31–2, 68–9
Oxford English Dictionary 71

parochialism 73–5, 87
parody 5
particular 66–8
Pascal, Blaise 99
Passions of the Soul, The 8
peditology 47–50, 109
perversion 104–5
Petronius 32
phenomenology 3–6, 20, 65–6, 88–91
physics 43–5, 50–1, 60, 109
Plato 2–3
Plessner, Helmuth 8–9, 28–9, 109
Plutarch 58
Pope, Alexander 15, 31
Porphyry 25
post-colonial theory 41–52
Powers, Austin 106
Praise of Folly 16

Protestantism 83
Proust 105
Prozac 102
psychoanalysis 102–4
Pythagoras 25

Quintillian 2

Rabelais, François 9, 25, 46, 109
Rabelais and his World 82–3
racism 6, 12, 66
Radio Éireann 110
raillery 81
reactionary humour 11–12
Red Cross 110
Reich, Annie 104
relativity 74–5, 79
relief theory 2–3
Renaissance 9, 83
repression 3, 12, 75–6, 82, 96
ridicule 11–12, 72; *sensus communis*
    81; super-ego 94–9, 103, 107,
    111
rire, Le 4, 55
risus purus 49, 109–11
rites 5, 10
Roman de Renard, Le 29

Samsa, Gregor 32
satire 31, 35–6, 72, 83
Satyricon 32
scapegoating 12, 76
scatology 45–7
Scheler, Max 42
Schopenhauer, Arthur 3
Schutz, Alfred 80, 86
Screech, M. A. 16, 26
Self, Will 31–3, 44–5
senescence 51

Sennett, Mack 57
sensus communis 18–20, 79–91
sexism 12, 74
sexuality 96
Shaftesbury, Anthony, Earl of 18,
    80–4
shaggy dog stories 7, 29
situation change 9–11
situationism 11
slavery 82
Smart, Christopher 30
smiling 5, 27–8, 107–9, 111
social contract 5
sociology 2
Socrates 25
solipsism 86
souls 45–50
Spencer, Herbert 3
Spengler, Oswald 83
Stalinism 83
Statius 38
Sterne, Laurence 16, 20–2, 73,
    106
stoicism 49
structured fun 12–14
subversion 82
super-ego 93–111
superiority theory 2–3, 70, 95–6
surrealism 10, 35
Swift, Jonathan 14–16, 31, 35–6;
    ethnicity 72–3; post-colonial
    theory 45, 47; *sensus communis*
    85; super-ego 106

theology 2, 25–6, 82
theories of humour 2–3, 18,
    88–9, 95
Theory of Communicative Action, The 87

thereness 86–7
thrownness 12, 75
Times Literary Supplement, The 47–8
timing 6–7
tomfoolery 83
totalitarianism 82
transference 103
Tristram Shandy 7, 20–2, 50

unconscious 3, 55, 93–111
United States 13
universalism 86
urbanity 31–4

Valéry, Paul 67
vices 15

Vico, Giambattista 80
Victoria, Queen 80
Virgin Mary 25–6
Voltaire 72
Vorticism 58

Waters, Eddie 9–10, 11
Watt 109–10
Wilde, Oscar 73
William III, King 82
Williams, Kenneth 43, 52
Wittgenstein, Ludwig 4, 18, 35, 86, 89, 99
Wodehouse, P. G. 11
World of Jeeves, The 11